ENNOBLING BUSINESS FOR SUCCESS

INSPIRE-IGNITE-INFLUENCE

DR. KASTHURI HENRY, PH.D
#1 INTERNATIONAL BEST SELLING AUTHOR

KasHenry Inc.
Steering Your Business for Success

Ennobling Business for Success
Inspire-Ignite-Influence

ISBN 978-1-7359555-5-1 (paperback)
ISBN 978-1-7359555-6-8 (hardcover)

Visit us online at www.kashenry.com
Printed in the United States of America.

WHAT PEOPLE ARE SAYING

"Each chapter ends by summarizing three key points, allowing for an easy read and reference for the impactful future work."
- *Mike Taney*, Chief Human Resources Officer, Duracell – A Berkshire Hathaway Company

"Push everything to the side because this is the book you have been waiting for. A highly relevant tome of useful thought and action for our world today."
- *Dr. Louise Mahler*. International Speaker, Executive Team Mentor & Executive Coach, Australia.

"Packed with practical wisdom and actionable strategies, this book is a must-read for all those who seek to tap into their full potential and create their own unique definition of success."
- *Nim Gholkar*. Author, Speaker, Life Coach, Australia.

"Living purpose is possible! Dr. Henry has created a must-read for those struggling to find meaning in the business world."
- *Charlotte Allen*, PhD. CEO, Rebel Success for Leaders, USA.

"This anthology is a genuine testimony that evolving together is possible, whatever our differences in our cultures, educations, backgrounds, and life choices."
- *Sophie Roumeas*. Therapist in hypnosis & family constellation, author, France.

"Kasthuri Henry has gathered a collection of stories rife with lessons to illuminate a path to more ethical, positive leadership. This is an essential read for today's leaders."
- *Liz Corcoran*. Senior Vice President, Design, Impact Performance Group, USA.

"Working collaboratively as a wholesome community is the recipe for success as the global pandemic has shown us. We have our inner truth to tap into and thrive."
- *Cruz Oliverio Gamez*. Managing Director, Gama Financial Services Ltd, Belize.

"This collection of carefully and brilliantly chosen people, and meticulously thought through chapters, written with the sole purpose of Inspiring, Igniting, and Influencing organizations and individuals, is in itself a very clever masterstroke."
- *Catherine Rolt*. Integrated Chinese Medical Consultant, CEO of UnRavel Dis-Ease Naturally Ltd, UK.

"This book is life-changing as it shares soulful, moral guidance and experiences from individuals from different backgrounds and occupations."
- *Anna Rachel Montejo*. Attorney at Law, Belize,

"*Ennobling Business for Success* is a book that disrupts the current paradigm of how business is done. Reading the perspective of Dr. Kasthuri along with the authors led me to the conclusion that people no longer want a separation between work and life. There is simply life."
- *Linda C Heeler, PCC*. USA.

"*Ennobling Business for success* is a must-read collection of inspiring thought leadership from many authors. It lays out a blueprint of how to create a brighter future in business while helping us become better in our everyday lives."
- *Hieu Bui, MD MBA FACHE*. USA.

"The ability to identify one's own purpose and build it as a leadership skillset can be a great challenge to most. The authors individually and collectively help you to learn more from their respective non-linear journey and the value they bring in life and work."
- *Kevyn Rustici*. Area Vice President - Strategic Human Capital Consultant

"Each chapter is a gift that helps you understand and unfold your own success by tapping into WHO you are, HOW you think, and WHAT you bring into the world. It's a must-read! "
- *Barbara Miller*. Leadership & Life Coach, and Author. Mighty Inspiration, LLC, USA.

"I would recommend this inspiring book to anyone seeking new, effective blueprints to establish their business, or to move forward with one in a post-pandemic world."
- *MacKenzie Nelson*, #1 International Best-Selling Author,

"*Ennobled Business for Success* brings transformational leadership into the world of corporate America. An enlightening read that sources input not often heard from our right brain colleagues."
- *Maureen Ryan Blake*. Maureen Ryan Blake Media Production, USA.

CONTENTS

Part Three: Influence by Design to Thrive

FOREWORD
ARJUN NAGENDRAN
CO-FOUNDER, MURSION

We live in a time where human connections are critically important in shaping the future of our world. The collective actions of humans have led to climate change and global warming, cultural and religious conflicts, socio-economic divides, inequitable societies, a raging pandemic, and a phenomenon now termed as "the Great Resignation," which deserves its own paragraph in this foreword. Our opinionated differences about these issues have been amplified over the last two decades with the rise of unregulated information disseminated primarily via social media, threatening to hamper the progress made by previous generations. It can be argued that many of these issues are avoidable if we learnt to be more collaborative, respectful, receptive, understanding, and empathetic towards our fellow human beings. It is only when we learn to understand human nature at its core, both individually and collectively, that I believe we can begin to make progress towards stemming these tides.

The world experienced something only imaginable by Hollywood when the pandemic surfaced. The pandemic highlighted some of the starkest differences in opinions of people while also causing seismic shifts in the way organizations were structured and run. There were some incredible positives when we came together and developed a vaccine in record time while hunkering down to reduce the spread of the contagion. However, it is hard to ignore the number of lives taken by the virus, particularly those that were lost due to the polarized nature of our societies and their beliefs. In this pandemic era, remote work and the creation of geographically distributed workforces saw a steep increase. This meant that there were more job opportunities in favorable conditions leading to mass exodus of people from their current roles in search of new ones where the "grass was greener." This phenomenon, rightly dubbed as "the Great Resignation,"[1] continues as the world embraces the changes that were forced upon it as a result of the pandemic. World-leading organizations have recognized that increased economic gains can be realized while still allowing the workforce to have flexible working routines. The biggest challenge facing these organizations today is how they can keep their multi-cultural, multi-geographical, remote workforces engaged, connected, and collaborative when the physical aspect of being social at work has been largely taken away.

To overcome these challenges, we are seeing the rapid adoption of immersive and connective technologies such as virtual reality and artificial intelligence. However, for people to truly feel connected and collaborative, the first and foremost component remains the human element. Technologies are only meant to augment and amplify our humanness. They are not substitutes and replacements for the things that only we (humans) can do well. Being kind, empathetic, transparent, malleable, and still being task- and goal-oriented is not something that comes naturally to all of us. Yet, we are expected to display these qualities in all aspects of our lives, none more so than in our respective lines of professional work. Despite the importance of these essential human skills to an organization's success, they are rarely taught in the workplace. I believe the best organizations of the future will recognize the need to cultivate these qualities in their workforces by giving deliberate thought to the types of professional development they offer within their departments. Employees will commit to an organization's growth only when they are supremely confident that their employer is as invested in their individual growth and success as the organization's own bottom line. The symbiotic relationship between employees and their employers has never been more critical than in this period of the Great Resignation. This work must begin at the top of every organization with caring, empathetic, and visionary leaders who realize that the strongest assets in an organization are their people and hence, choose to invest in their personal growth.

---

[1] https://www.mga.edu/news/2022/04/what-is-the-great-resignation.php

Mursion, the company I co-founded, was created with one vision—to help people understand and shape their own behaviors in a safe and simulated environment. The primary objective of the simulation platform is to help us all be better prepared to handle difficult situations in the real world while mitigating unintended negative consequences that may occur as a result of our inexperience. In my role as Mursion's Chief Technology Officer, I spend most of my time studying novel empathic technologies and exploring their future capability in unlocking human potential. Mursion uses the power of virtual reality and artificial intelligence to create highly immersive safe spaces where natural human interactions can occur in a variety of high stakes real world scenarios. When this interaction data is carefully analyzed, we begin to notice patterns and aspects of human behavior that may be subconscious in nature, yet affect the outcome of these conversational exchanges. In daily life, this amounts to the things we say or do that may unknowingly result in strained human relations. It is hard enough to consciously build, foster, and sustain human relationships that are so critical to both our personal and professional lives. Add to this the complex nature of our subconscious, and the size of the task at hand in alleviating the aforementioned global issues suddenly seems much more daunting.

What resonates with me about Dr. Kasthuri's approach, wonderfully described in her book *Ennobled For Success*, is her deliberate and thoughtful guidance on understanding the complex nature of human interactions and our individual purpose. Mursion's vision and mission statements are closely aligned with Kasthuri's work, allowing us to cross paths during many professional events. In the short time that I've known her, it is easy to notice these values manifesting themselves during our interactions. From self-awareness to conscious listening to unconscious bias, Kasthuri breaks down the importance of our own characteristics, and the associated science that can help us be happier and successful while infectiously spreading the same spirit among others. Her inspiring and personable storytelling reminds me of the "man in the mirror"—we only need to look at ourselves to make the most meaningful and impactful changes around us. Her attention and skill at forging deep human relationships has allowed Kasthuri to create a wonderful compilation of chapters written by international leaders from various organizations. This anthology, focused on building societies and workplaces enriched by collaborative and emotionally intelligent people, is sure to make a deep connection to your personal and professional life, no matter where you may be on this journey.

Arjun Nagendran is the Co-Founder, Chief Technology Officer, and Head of Research and Development at Mursion®, Inc., a San Francisco based startup specializing in the application of artificial intelligence and virtual reality to positively influence human collaboration.

Arjun completed his Ph.D. in Robotics from the University of Manchester, UK, specializing in landing mechanisms for Unmanned Air Vehicles. Prior to Mursion, he worked for several years as an academic researcher, contributing to several projects including the development of a robot to explore the Great Egyptian Pyramid, surveillance robots for the UK Ministry of Defense, and real-time robotic control systems to catch fast-moving objects. He holds several patents and has won numerous awards for advances in technology. Throughout his career, he has been the recipient of research and development fundings from the Office of Naval Research, Bill & Melinda Gates Foundation, National Science Foundation, and others. He has served on the organizing committee and as a reviewer for several conferences and journals including the International Conference on Intelligent Robots and Systems (IROS), International Conference on Advances in Computer Entertainment Technology (ACE), IEEE International Symposium on Mixed and Augmented Reality (ISMAR), Robotica, Advanced Robotics, Virtual Reality Journal, Entertainment Computing Journal, and the IEEE Aerospace and Electronic Systems Magazine Online Journal. Arjun's current portfolio includes coupling artificial intelligence, human psychology and learning sciences with technological innovations in remote-operation, virtual and augmented reality, and control system theory to create high-impact real world applications.

Email Address: arjun.nagendran@mursion.com
Website:www.arjunnagendran.com
LinkedIn Page:www.linkedin.com/in/arjunnagendran

PREFACE
By Dr. Kasthuri Henry, PhD

*"Challenges come our way to strengthen us and polish our souls to seek great-**ness**. Giving into struggles is not what the human journey is about. It is about building resiliency to use the roadblocks as steppingstones and see the silver lining in each cloud. Success is forged by continuous polishing and never giving up on ourselves and others around us."*
—Dr. Kasthuri Henry, Ennobled for Success, From Civil War to a US CFO, Oct 2020

The world around us is rapidly evolving at previously unheard-of speed and evolve with it, we must. Evolving to remain relevant is a necessity. The guidance for this journey of intentional evolution comes from knowing, understanding, and living our purpose. *Our purpose remains the true north of our transformation, when we mindfully navigate life even during turbulent times.* The global pandemic has created the situation where every person around the world had the opportunity to take an introspective journey into their own life, work, and relationships to ponder their purpose and where the road forward was. This is such a transformative period offering each one of us the perfect opportunity to choose our paths; not just the road we take, but how we take it as a whole person with our heart, mind, body, and spirit intact.

The Great Resignation[2] seen in the workplace is the direct result of employees seeing how they are not valued by employers. *Failing to create an authentic sense of belonging to lay the foundation for inclusion is the lasting failure of most employers as they have historically rushed to build a profit-motivated transactional workplace*

---

[2]   Parker, Kim and Menasce Horowitz, Juliana. Majority of workers who quit a job in 2021 cite low pay, no opportunities for advancement, feeling disrespected. Pew Research Center. March 9, 2022. Downloaded from https://www.pewresearch.org/fact-tank/2022/03/09/majority-of-workers-who-quit-a-job-in-2021-cite-low-pay-no-opportunities-for-advancement-feeling-disrespected/

culture. A culture of disposable workforce rotating in and out through the proverbial revolving door. When workers evaluated their life purpose and determined their self-worth, they saw emerging opportunities in the rapidly growing *work from anywhere* global workplace culture[3] that allowed them to harmonize life by balancing paid and unpaid work that is involved with human existence while making happiness the center of career choices. The realities that were ignored prior to the pandemic became the center of focus and the workplace had to transform to meet the call of our times. That workplace transformation opened the door for workers to seek value-congruent prospects. The pandemic has also taught workers to become more self-reliant, giving them the courage to choose what is in their self-interest. *Now, employers need to learn to embrace the human spirit and cultivate a culture of belonging while being purpose driven if they are to attract and retain talent that will innovate and grow their organization.*

As I saw the opportunities that lie ahead, I also realized that there will be a need for guidance for those individuals and organizations who need to lean in. As a nurturing global business leader and graduate school professor, who values the potential of every soul to live their full life, I believe in providing multiple sources of guidance for my students and teams. Co-creating an anthology to ennoble businesses for success seemed a divine idea, giving me the momentum to seek out international leaders who valued the human experience. Born of this intentionality is this anthology, focused on the human skills necessary for organizations to cultivate a sustainable culture rooted in humanity. *The soul of an organization is the character of that organization. From that organizational character stems the behaviors, values, and actions that drives the organizational economic engine. Since excellence is a habit demonstrated by consistent behavior, the human capital attraction and development becomes the new frontier of organizational excellence.*

Selecting the authors to contribute to this anthology has been an ennobling experience unto itself. Building the shared purpose, establishing the process without compromising the individual spirit of the authors, cultivating an environment of collaboration beyond the chapter writing to create a lived experience of ennobling one another, and holding space for life as it transpired over the course of eight months have all been fulfilling to me, as the coach and compiler. The honor to have the trust of these amazing international professionals, guiding their unique voices and messages to be visible in the world stage, and bringing this anthology forward has been a humbling experience. My heart is

---

[3] Choudhury, Prithwiraj (Raj). *Our Work-from-Anywhere Future.* Harvard Business Review, Nov-Dec 2020. Downloaded from https://hbr.org/2020/11/our-work-from-anywhere-future

filled with gratitude for each contributing author and their purpose-filled message that will help transform businesses and set them up for success.

I could not have had a more meaningful foreword writer than Arjun Nagendran, co-founder of Mursion. His purpose-driven life work of integrating robotics and artificial intelligence to improve the human experience as well as overcome implicit bias is cutting-edge work. A serendipitous business connection following the launch of my book, *Ennobled for Success, From Civil War to a US CFO*, has blossomed into a personal and professional relationship proving that our authentic, shared experiences have the power to transcend all else. I encourage you, as the reader, to explore the beauty of technology and humanity ennobling each other instead of being perceived as being at cross-purposes with each other. *Just shifting our perspective slightly has the power to catapult us to unlocking our innate greatness.*

Written words have the power to move generations to come. This anthology contains three sections, each intentionally selected to be a part of the Ennobled for Success ™ brand.

1. *Inspire:* Inspire the human spirit so each soul feels valued and could live its full potential.
2. *Ignite:* Ignite the sense of purpose to mindfully build a fulfilling life.
3. *Influence:* Influence by design to thrive and leave a legacy of ennobling.

As part of the Ennobled for Success ™ Series, Ennobling Business for Success is brought forward by Ennobled for Success ™ Publishing to ensure value congruence of the message, process, and the whole lived experience. Ennobled for Success ™ Institute is part of the portfolio offerings for a guided learning and development continuum to continually develop the human skills necessary for building organizational and societal experiences by design with intentionality. *We have the opportunity to leave this place we call earth better than we found it and I invite you to come aboard to take the co-creative ride. A ride of our shared purpose. A ride of our shared humanity. A ride of our shared happiness*

PART ONE

Inspire the Human Spirit

GRATITUDE AS A LIFESTYLE
BY WOLFGANG TRAMPE

Why Am I Thankful?

Let me start with a short story. It was a chilly Saturday morning and the aircraft engine was humming as it approached the airport. Suddenly the engine stopped—dead silence. The small Cessna started descending rapidly as the pilot prepared himself and his passenger for the crash. The plane was destroyed, but both occupants survived with minor injuries. The pilot was my father, and I was the passenger. This happened as I had just turned 18 with my whole adult life in front of me; it could have ended then. As we crashed, I didn't make deals with God, just asked that He show me His purpose for me should I survive.

We all have those inflection points in our lives, whether an accident, a family death, illness, marriage, divorce, or other events that, if we survive them, give us a chance to evaluate our lives and decide how we are going to move forward. I chose to be thankful.

Gratitude is not an attitude as many say, but a lifestyle, one that must be intentionally practiced until it becomes a habit. It can take on many forms or expressions—in my case, I chose to serve. I learned from my parents that service to others is the best expression of gratitude because it shows that you are content with what you have (much or little) and are willing to share with others, whether it is your time, your resources, or other things of value. I have heard that gratefulness is key to happiness, peace, and joy, and I believe it.

Embracing My Purpose

Now, as an HR executive after 30+ years in the corporate world, nothing has really changed. My life's journey has taught me that being thankful every day for everything I have—the good and the bad, the small and the big—opens my heart to serving others and making their day special. I read somewhere that we should not conform to this world (or to our situation), but we must transform ourselves by the renewing of our minds (Romans 12:2). So, we must make a conscious decision to be thankful and serve others, every day.

I am thankful for my God, who has provided for all my needs. He gave me my wife, my daughter, and my extended family, for which I am very thankful. When I was a child, we (my sisters and I) didn't have much (as the world measures) but we had loving parents that cared for us, fed us, corrected us, guided us, and taught us the values we espouse today. They worked hard to give us a good education, which has opened several doors in our lives. They walk along with us; in Spanish we have a saying "*nos encaminaron,*" which basically means they walked with us until we were ready to run on our own.

I apply similar principles in my daily walk. There are so many people who not only need someone to walk along with them in their journey, they need support, guidance, and sometimes even a little kick in the back side to move along. That is what I believe to be my purpose.

Modeling Gratitude Through Service

A few years ago, I had a pause in my corporate work life, so I took the opportunity to serve while I searched for my next corporate job. I had recently attended culinary school, so I became a cook in a homeless shelter. I not only cooked for them but also spent time sitting down, sharing the meal, and listening to their stories. Eventually this opportunity grew into running a program

INSPIRE THE HUMAN SPIRIT

where I taught them basic cooking and serving skills, gave them practice via a catering operation, and then helped to place them in hospitality jobs. God gave me a chance to use my skills (HR, cooking, and problem solving) in serving others and walking along with them in their journey.

So, what can you, dear reader, do as a leader in your daily walk? Whether at home, workplace, or your community. I don't have all the answers, but I can offer you a few suggestions:

Serve your organization. That does not mean bringing cookies every day (although that would be good occasionally), but take the time to get to know the people you work with individually. Understand where they came from, where they are in their journey, and where they want to go. Understand what is important to them, what motivates them to jump out of bed every day and give their best and, most importantly, how you can walk along with them and help remove barriers, provide coaching and resources, so that they can become all that they want to be. People will always remember how you made them feel when you do this for them, and most importantly, they will want to do the same for others.

Leave people with a good flavor in their mouth. Again, not talking about food here but I do want to use a food example. I am a good cook and have won a few chili-cooking contests in my day. One time there was a dinner at our local church where everyone brought their best chili. One gentleman who had tried my cooking before asked me which one was my chili, so I showed him and he served himself. But I noticed that he was not trying my chili during the evening so I asked him why. He said to me, "I want to have your chili last because I want your food to be the last flavor I have in my mouth when I go home." Make sure that whatever you do for your organization you do it with passion and excellence, so that they will walk away with a good taste and will want more.

Start your day giving thanks and asking guidance on how to better serve others. Every day has its own problems, so I pray to my God to guide my steps on how to better help a specific person or group. If you are content with what you have, then it is much easier to be thankful for the good things and for the bad things, and then you are free to serve. I have my own beliefs guided by my Christian upbringing, but I know that many other beliefs speak of service and gratitude as well.

- *Islam:* There is a verse in the Quran that reminds believers to be grateful. It says, "And whatever of blessings and good things you have, it is from Allah" (16:53).

- *Hinduism:* One of the tenants of the Hinduism is "Dharma," the sacred duty of life, and it encompasses ten forms of duty including duty towards fellow human beings, duty towards other living beings, duty towards society, moral duty, professional duty, and duty towards other faiths (https://www.hinduwebsite.com/buzz/the-ten-main-duties-in-hinduism.asp). Fulfilling the duty of life, therefore, is in the service to all living beings, including society and profession, mindfully upholding the moral duty, making *service to man is service to God* a way of life.
- *Judaism:* "Acts of kindness never die. They linger in the memory, giving life to other acts in return" (Jonathan Sacks, in *From Optimism to Hope*). This wise observation echoes the Jewish realization that mitzvah goreret mitzvah: one good deed begets another. (https://www.aish.com/ci/s/10-Jewish-Quotes-About-Kindness.html)

Impact of Gratitude On Becoming an Influential Servant Leader

Be thankful for your current business situation: Whether great or not so good, you are a Leader and were placed here for a reason and for a season. What a great opportunity to serve your team and coach them into delivering the strong business results that are expected of you. Also, what an opportunity to showcase your skills as a caring leader and problem solver.

Be thankful for your team: As a Leader you have been entrusted with the livelihoods and careers of your team members. We do not always get a chance to choose our team. You will have strong team members, those who you can point in the right direction, get out of their way, and they will "take the hill." You will also have those team members that will need additional coaching and directing. To me, those are particularly satisfying to lead because of the joy and satisfaction on their faces when they learn a new relevant skill, complete the task, or improve their performance.

Be thankful for the achievement of results: Celebrate small wins along the way and any big milestones. This will reinforce to the team that you are all heading in the right direction and will support any learning (process or skills) they have obtained along the way. Make sure you celebrate once you and your team have achieved the required business result. And in the end, take time to thank the higher being that placed you there, gave you the team to work with, and allowed you to achieve the great results you are now celebrating.

I'd like to leave you with a few verses that guide my behavior and encourage my daily walk. They come from the book of Philippians in the Christian bible: ". . . for I have learned to be content whatever the circumstances. I know what it is to be in need, and I know what it is to have plenty. I have learned the secret of being content in any and every situation, whether well fed or hungry, whether living in plenty or in want. I can do all this through Him who gives me strength" (4:11-13).

May you be blessed by these words from a humble servant.

Wisdom Gained from the Journey to Ennoble Business

1. Understand your role as a leader and be thankful you were placed there for a particular reason and season.
2. Value your team members and commit to making them stronger than when you got them.
3. Always celebrate and be thankful for the results achieved and the team that enabled the results.

Wolfgang Trampe is a Human Resources executive with 30+ years of corporate experience with Global Companies. His life's purpose is to serve others, from helping develop corporate leadership teams, coaching emerging leaders, and providing for his family and his Church, to providing nourishing meals to the homeless. Born and raised in Guatemala, Wolfgang grew up in a stable home with loving parents and two sisters. He studied in the United States and received degrees in both Management Information Systems and Electrical Engineering, after which he started his corporate career in a Fortune 100 company as an Automation and Controls Engineer in manufacturing facilities. His work with people in manufacturing confirmed Wolfgang's calling to serve people through a career shift to Human Resources.

In HR, Wolfgang has worked to improve Talent Acquisition and Talent Development systems as well as developing effective Leadership Teams that deliver strong business results. Wolfgang thrives on partnering with business Leaders to coach them to improve their leadership effectiveness that translates into great organizational and business results. Wolfgang also has passion for food and for feeding people. He studied and obtained a Culinary Arts certificate from the Midwest Culinary Institute in Cincinnati.

Wolfgang's main theme in life is Gratefulness, from surviving a tragic accident as a teenager to being blessed by having a beautiful family (wife and daughter) and having the privilege of coaching and enabling others to improve their lives and careers thought his HR and culinary work.

Email: wolfgangtrampe27@gmail.com
LinkedIn: www.linkedin.com/in/wolfgangtrampe
Twitter: @ChefWolfman

THE JOURNEY OF FAILURE
AND SELF-DISCOVERY:
THE HEART OF A MUSICIAN
BY DR. CHERYL LENTZ

Failure is often an ominous word, one that implies pain, fear, and judgment. It is the one word that stops people in their tracks. **FEAR**, quite simply, is **F**alse **E**vidence **A**ppearing **R**eal. We believe. We buy into it. We allow the fear of failure to dictate our journey and invade our thoughts. We need to stop. Today. The purpose of this writing is to reframe how we think about the fear of failure, its function, and the gift that failure offers in our pursuit of success. If we cannot learn to fail and process the gifts of failure, we will never learn to truly succeed.

Mastery

Malcolm Gladwell says it takes 10,000 hours to achieve mastery. Mastery takes time, skill, patience, perseverance, conviction, and commitment. Many simply do not have what it takes to go that distance. Instead, we stop. We shut

ENNOBLING BUSINESS FOR SUCCESS

down. We avoid so we do not have to feel the pain that failure often brings. Because of the pain, we often miss our greatest gifts and opportunities.

Mastery means we need to do the work of learning *first*. We do not come out of the womb walking; we must learn. We appreciate the skill needed to *become* an expert; we don't want to go through the pain of learning to get there. We give up too soon, if we even have the courage to begin at all.

We need to make friends with failure; to celebrate failure. We need to recognize the importance and the gifts that failure offers, so we can learn how to fail with intention and gratitude.

Learning to Fail

Often, we embrace phrases like Apollo 13's *failure is not an option*. I disagree. Failure is the *only* option. Those engineers at NASA understood the outcome, but what they did not understand is that failure was the way to get there. I believe an expert is someone who knows failure, intimately, with skill, grace, and conviction. Edison knew failure wasn't a big deal. Failure was simply a process of systematic learning in inventing the lightbulb. Number 1 didn't work. Number 568 didn't work, neither did number 779, and on he went until, legend has it, number 998 was the magic number. Failure is the process, not the outcome.[4]

"Success is not final; failure is not fatal. It is the courage to continue that counts."
—Winston Churchill

Many simply let fear of the process stop them **from** attaining success. Edison kept going **until** success. The secret is in understanding and processing failure as a tool to get to the outcome, success for mastery.

---

[4]   Ramkumar N. (2019, December 21). "The greatest inventor, Thomas Alva Edison's vision on failures." https://www.linkedin.com/pulse/greatest-inventor-thomas-alva-edisons-vision-failures-narayanan/

The Magic of Failure

Few people may ever truly understand the magic of failure. Once you unlock its secrets, one learns to **fail faster, to succeed sooner**, to get to the good stuff. The question is how. The key is to focus on learning as a game and as a process; failure is simply feedback that something didn't work.

We cannot take failure personally. Herein lies the magic: learning to separate yourself, **the person,** from yourself, **the skill.** We are not our failure. Failure is neither a destination nor an outcome, it is simply a process.

An elegant example is a child learning to walk. It's a game. A child simply observes the world around them and sees people getting places faster with their legs. *Hmm.* They decide to try this walking thing. They get up, they try, they fall. Boom. Failure.

What do they do next?

They giggle. They learn in that moment what **not** to do. They get up, they try again. This time, they go backwards; they lose their balance and fall. They recover, realizing: *Nope, that didn't work. Let's try something else.* They keep getting up, remembering what **not** to do the next time **until** they hit on the magic combination. Bingo! They stumble on the elegance of learning; expertise comes from getting it wrong first. An expert is simply someone who learned what not to do along those 10,000 hours until they got it right. Until the lightbulb turned on. Until they learned to walk.

Simple? Maybe.

Easy? It depends on attitude.

Edison understood. There weren't any expectations of how long the process might take. The lightbulb would work when it worked, not a moment sooner. Edison followed the process of trying something, failing, eliminating, and trying something else. He kept a record of what didn't work. He kept going. He knew the process. He learned. Rinse. Repeat.

Failure Has No Alibi

The process is Try. Do. Do it again. And again. And again . . . however long it takes for success. Many give up too soon. Napoleon Hill has a phrase: *Failure Has No Alibi.* We must own our failures. We cannot hide. We must understand and own the process. Failure isn't who we are; failure is the process of learning until we succeed. No big deal, right? For some.

For others, failure shuts them down. Failure produces fear: fear of what people might say. Fear of what we might say to ourselves. Fear of not being good enough, of not being enough. Failure is a mindset that needs to be understood and overcome.

Failure Is Painful

We like when we get it right. We like mastery. We like **being** the expert. We don't often like the work required in **becoming** one.

I am a musician. It takes courage to admit that as I had not played in 35 years because of one of my epic failures. When I was told for the **first** time I wasn't good enough by my professor in college, I stopped playing. I heard I wasn't good enough and I should find another line of work. I did. I believed him. I stopped playing that day. I gave away my music and walked away from a significant part of me. This was the day the music died.

That wasn't the end of the story. Music kept trying to find me. Sadly, I didn't listen. I didn't hear the messenger. God kept my gift until I was ready, however. I walked away because it was too painful to play and too painful to have someone judge me as not good enough.

What I *should* have heard was that I was not *as good as*. I should have found a mentor to understand the gift of failure. The failure wasn't that I wasn't good enough or not as good as, but that I stopped playing because I wasn't strong enough to keep going. The pain was too much to find another way. I could have made different choices. He was right that I was not as talented as the graduate students who were amazingly brilliant. While I might not have achieved their greatness, I had my own gift to give and share with the world in my own way. Instead, I walked.

After 35 years, I tried again. On Valentine's Day 2022, in Prince of Peace Church, I fell back in love . . . with my music and me. I had the courage to try. The Music Director allowed the privilege to see if I had any magic still in me.

I cried the night before. I cried on the way to the church. I cried as I put my organ shoes on. I cried as I placed my fingers on the keyboards. I felt the music come forth once again . . . from the depth of my soul that had been kept under lock and key for more than three decades. I met my destiny once again. I released the pain that kept the love of my life from me. I let go and lost myself in the music all over again. For several amazing hours, my fingers danced across the keyboards and my feet across the pedals. I had finally conquered my mountain.

The question everyone asks is whether I was any good. That didn't matter. I was thrilled just to have the ability to try and invite music back into my life. There was talent there, but it will take time to nurture. I am not as good as I once was. The question I needed to answer was whether I was willing to meet my love and gift of music again and pick up where I left off. I chose courage to unlock my soul and let my heart sing.

The Music Director listened to every klunker and every wrong note I played. But that's not what he heard. What he saw was the joy on my face as my body, heart, mind, and soul came together as one for the first time in more than three decades. I was flying higher than I had been in my life. He said we should all be so lucky to have such talent after 35 years. I smiled. It was a start. My gift was still there. The magic was still in me. Now the choice was mine as to what to do next.

The Heart of a Musician

I will forever be grateful for both gifts: the day I stopped playing (my life moved in an unexpected direction on a journey that looked vastly different than what I anticipated) and the day I started playing again.

I've had an amazing career. The universe needed me along a different path to touch those who needed my other gifts. Now it is time to come home. Music is back, and I have the honor and privilege of self-discovery to make another choice and fall back in love with me and my music.

As a college professor, I teach the benefits of authentic leadership with learning to embrace who we are and how to process failure along the way, to understand what happens physically, emotionally, mentally, spiritually, and professionally, particularly when we walk away from our purpose. As an academic, I spent far too many years listening to my head—the intellectual, the logic, the expected, always taking the safer and easier path, listening to those ahead of me thinking they knew best. They didn't.

I finally moved into my heart to feel every glorious misstep, every time I fell, every time I gave up. I am grateful for every missed opportunity and every broken path that led me to where I find myself today. The gifts are amazing despite the pain. I rediscovered that within me lies the heart and soul of a musician. Being a musician is not what I do, it is who I am to my very core. I found my way back home and I intend never to leave again.

My purpose is back. Music fills me up, connecting me to and with the world. Slowly the world showed the options I could have **if** I had the courage to believe and dare to dream again. I could make a different choice. It is never too late. I shifted my path to resume my journey despite the 35 year detour.

Many lack the courage to take this new path. Why? I have been a college professor for 22 years. I know how to do what I do. I have more than 10,000 hours as the expert, knowing what works and what doesn't. I have accomplishments of multiple publications, multiple doctoral graduates, having taught more than 10,000 students during my career, a TEDx Talk, with radio, podcasts, and speaking around the world. I have been truly blessed. The challenge is that when we learn something new, we often must start over. It is humbling to begin again and dare to take a new path forward.

Advice to Our Younger Selves

I asked a friend of mine if he had the chance to go back to give himself advice, what he would say. I was shocked at his answer. He said he would tell his younger self not a darn thing. Really? Nothing? He explained that who he became was because of every broken road, every failure, every missed opportunity, and every painful moment that shaped him into the man who sat before me. I paused. I got the chills. I realized he was right. I spent a lifetime with this regret, wishing I could have told my younger self all kinds of things. Instead, my desire is to wish her a fabulous adventure and to tell her to believe in herself and not let failure stop her, wherever it led, to just keep going.

Conclusion

Failure is not final unless we decide it is and we stop trying. Failure is simply that friend that encourages us to keep trying something else until we get it right. Find your voice and your inner guide to forge your own path to learn to create your own wisdom and then share with others. We often create and perpetuate this culture of failure. We need to stop, break the cycle, and love ourselves even more through every misstep. We need to smile and look back at what a marvelous journey it has been.

I would not change a thing.

Wisdom Gained from the Journey to Ennoble Business

1. Failure is not who we are.
2. Failure is not a destination.
3. Failure is not the outcome.
4. Failure is part of the process.
5. Fail faster, succeed sooner.

Dr. Cheryl Lentz, known as the Academic Entrepreneur, is a unique and dynamic speaker who intensely connects with her audience, having one foot in academia and one foot in the business and entrepreneurial space. Her goal is to offer the audience pearls of wisdom today they can use tomorrow in their personal and professional lives. It is not enough to know; the expectation is for participants to take action and do. Join Dr. Cheryl on her journey to connect these dots to provide inspiration, knowledge, and counsel to move forward effectively.

Known globally for her writings on leadership and failure, as well as critical and refractive thinking, she has been published more than 52 times with 26 writing awards. As an accomplished university professor, speaker, & consultant, she is an international best-selling author, and top quoted publishing professional on ABC, CBS, NBC, and Fox. She took the stage as a TEDx Speaker in *Farningdale2020, October 10, 2020.

http://refractivethinker.com/authors/dr-cheryl-a-lentz/
https://www.amazon.com/Cheryl-Lentz/e/B002D63EPC
https://twitter.com/DrCherylLentz
https://www.facebook.com/successthroughfailure/
https://www.facebook.com/Dr.Cheryl.Lentz
https://www.linkedin.com/in/drcheryllentz/
https://www.youtube.com/drcheryllentz
https://www.instagram.com/drcheryllentz/
http://www.DrCherylLentz.com
email: drcheryllentz@gmail.com

ACCELERATE YOUR SUCCESS
BY CREATING YOUR OWN POWER TRIBE
BY LINDA FISK

I believe my purpose is to accelerate the success of women in leadership around the world, by connecting them to the resources, networks, tools, experiences, diagnostics, and relationships that advance their unique purpose. In fact, creating a confidential and supportive community designed to accelerate success of each member by integrating self-directed learning, impactful group experiences, peer advisory services, and expert-led coaching and mentoring is the highest value I can offer.

And, I believe it is more important than ever to be intentional about seeking out, investing in, and forming the kind of genuine and strategic relationships we need, as women in leadership, to thrive both personally and professionally.

High performing executives tend to value the perspectives of other leaders, as well as the wisdom that comes from the practical experiences learned by others in similar circumstances. But, most leaders don't have a "safe" environment where they can share their concerns. C-Suite executives often feel that any public show of vulnerability or uncertainty opens them up to significant risk: risk of losing the confidence or respect of their boards of directors, employees, or customers.

Being in a community of other leaders allows you to have an outlet to continuously learn and improve in a confidential setting and get exposure to new ways of approaching problems and issues, as well as new ways of leveraging opportunities. Importantly, this kind of safe, supportive environment allows members to develop friendships and networks with other women in leadership that can enrich their professional and personal lives.

Importantly, choosing a leadership community that supports your unique purpose can benefit both the leader that is focused on personal and professional development as well as the business they represent. Being an active participant in the kind of community that accelerates your success and advances your purpose supports the growth and profitability of your organization because you benefit from the hard-won lessons and experience of other leaders. **Members also have access to best practices on key issues, they can receive honest advice and feedback from peers who have no conflict of interest, and they can collaborate with other leaders to work "on" the business rather than "in" the business.** As Aristotle said, "Excellence is not an act, but a habit."

In fact, according to a recent study of Stein + Partners, members of leadership communities experienced average revenue growth rate just above 5% the prior year, compared to an industry average of only 1.62%—more than a 200% faster growth! And, executives who set aside the time to attend leadership learning events and leadership networking exchanges experienced dramatically superior operating results. In fact, members of these leadership organizations enjoyed operating margins of 22.6% in the prior year vs. an overall average of 10.26%—more than twice the profitability![5]

We know that leadership networks are critical to professional advancement. But research from The Kellogg School of Management at Northwestern University now tells us that men and women need different kinds of networks to succeed. Because women in executive leadership often face cultural and political hurdles that men typically do not, they benefit from an inner circle of close female contacts that can share private, confidential information. Women often face a greater challenge in networking to find professional opportunities and career advancement—and they, more than

---

[5]   Stein + Partners Study of Chief Executive Network Members vs. Their Industries

men, need to maintain both wide networks and informative inner circles in order to land the best position and secure the most advantageous opportunities. The good news is that by taking a smart approach, women can continue to find meaningful advancement options. Identifying and connecting with people who are connected to multiple networks is a key strategy. Build a large network, but have a close inner circle of women that support you, champion you, advise you, and encourage you.[6]

Being a part of a leadership community has significant, and proven, benefits. But, leadership communities are not for every executive. To benefit, you need to be:

- **Committed to improvement**
  Those who believe that holding a C-Suite title is the end of your learning journey should probably not participate. On the other hand, members who value continuous learning and believe every C-Suite leader must invest in their ongoing professional development can make excellent members.

- **Willing to make a time commitment**
  Consistent participation is often an important ingredient in bonding peers and building the trust required to discuss key issues. All C-Suite executives are busy, and prospective members in any group should view participation as a priority.

- **Be self-aware**
  In addition to improved organizational performance, successful members aim to increase levels of satisfaction and performance in their own work as well as that of their employees, their customers, and investors.

- **Have a sense of humility**
  Members must demonstrate a willingness to share their personal triumphs—and, as importantly—their failures. Hard-won experience (good and bad) is what provides depth and meaning for leaders of substance.

If you think that you are the kind of leader that would benefit from joining a dynamic leadership organization, there's never been a better time to invest in your success. Virtual networking allows for a customized approach to

---

[6]   The Economic Journal 2020; Kellogg School of Management at Northwestern University

networking. With flexible scheduling, the ability to access recordings, and the affordability factor, virtual networking can not only expand your leadership, but it can enhance your influence globally.

Here are a few tips to ensure that you get the most out of your leadership community, and create your own power tribe:

- **Carve out regularly scheduled time to review and grow your network.** Ready-built leadership communities makes it easy to reach out—and to ensure that you are optimizing your membership. Share often. Be a resource and expand your thought-leadership. Be an active and daily participant, leveraging touch points to maintain your existing connections and grow your network.

- **It's time to get comfortable being visible, because networking also involves being seen.** Ready to establish your expertise? Use your leadership community to leverage your thought leadership by sharing career related articles, posting current information and resource-rich content and asking questions. Participate in chat sessions and answer questions. Interacting consistently in these groups showcases your expertise while connecting you with others. If you own your own business and show up and participate in these groups, you'll be branding yourself as a thought leader. Be sure to join hosted roundtables or learning events through "live" sessions and recordings.

- **Attend community masterminds, roundtables, virtual webinars and summits.** Many in-person conferences, summits, and workshops are now offered through online platforms, offering you a cost-effective strategy to network without the expense of travel. Many of these online networking opportunities are strategically scheduled outside of normal business hours. Still can't make the live event? Register anyway—most times the host will give you access to the recording if you register.

Here are three reasons why joining and remaining active in a leadership community, and creating your own power tribe, should be at the top of your priority list:

- **Stay on top of your game.**
  Access to a group of unbiased, objective and successful leaders, working to solve any challenges you face, is priceless. Sure, if you spend a few weeks scouring the Internet, flipping through manuals, and binging on podcasts, you could figure just about anything out. But you don't have to go through all that time and trouble with an intelligent and passionate power tribe at your fingertips. Your leadership community cares about you, and their goal is to ensure your success.

- **Personal and professional growth.**
  No one grows as a leader without support from others. Find a leadership community where you can meet inspirational leaders, create lifelong friendships, and be surrounded by people that are invested in your success. You just might discover a new mentor, partner, or employee that can take you to the next level. To continue to advance in your success, it's important to find a supportive, trusting community where you can receive support from influential and highly connected business leaders that are helping you develop the strategies to pursue your passions and purpose, and dramatically increase your success.

- **Return the favor.**
  Creating your own power tribe through a leadership community affords you the chance to give back to others. As Zig Ziglar said, "You can get everything in life you want if you will just help enough other people get what they want." Plus, the only thing that feels better than accomplishing your goals is helping other leaders reach their goals.

Once you've identified the leadership community that is dedicated to accelerating your success and supports your unique purpose, it's important to *activate* your power tribe, which means being intentional about investing in these relationships.

<u>Here are a few tips for activating your leadership community and creating your own power tribe:</u>

- **Proactively pencil them in.**
  How often do we find ourselves saying, "Let's catch up soon," but then we fail to actually schedule the time to do so? One of the best things you can do is proactively schedule time with the people in your success circle.

Have a tough week ahead? Schedule some time to call one or two people from your re-energize group. Feeling challenged by a new work project and need some advice? It may be time to call your mentor.

- **Share your goals with them.**
  We all have things we want to achieve. One of the best ways to keep in touch with your success circle is to inform them of your goals. Not only is this going to help with accountability, but you would be surprised how people are able to help you when they understand what it is you want to accomplish. Be sure to ask them what their goals are, too, and how you might be able to support them and work together.

- **Make it a symbiotic relationship.**
  Don't hesitate to leverage your success circle when you need an "in" or introduction to someone outside of your network, keeping in mind that you also bring value to the relationship. Someone in your circle may come to you asking for a favor. If you aren't the person for the job, someone else in your success circle might be, so pass it on and share the wealth of your network with others.

I am honored and humbled to help inspirational women in leadership all over the world accelerate their success by defining their vision, growing their leadership, expanding their influence, and leaving a lasting legacy. **LeadHERship Global offers an impactful global community of extraordinary women, unleashing the full potential of high-performing and growth-oriented leaders in a confidential, supportive, and private community.**

LeadHERship Global offers women in leadership the opportunity to:

- Meet inspirational leaders, create lifelong friendships, and be surrounded by people who are invested in your success.
- You will be inspired and motivated by other women leaders who will cheer, counsel, and support you to greater levels of success and impact.
- The purpose of LeadHERship Global is to create and support personal and professional breakthroughs and guide women to achieving greater leverage and freedom in their careers and businesses.
- We provide a global community of world-class women thought leaders and experts brought together to collaborate and facilitate excellent outcomes for each other.

Wisdom Gained from the Journey to Ennoble Business

1. True success isn't based on whether you think you're winning or losing in the moment. Instead, success is consistently doing the work that ignites your soul.
2. Dedicate time this week to find the best leadership community for you. They will make invaluable allies along your journey.
3. It is more important than ever to be intentional about investing in and seeking out the right relationships we need to thrive both personally and professionally.

Linda Fisk is a multi-award-winning leader, keynote speaker, best-selling author and university professor dedicated to amplifying and extending the success of other high-caliber business leaders. She is the Founder and CEO of LeadHERship Global, a community of unstoppable women enhancing their leadership blueprint and embracing their power to be the best version of themselves—in work and life. In LeadHERship Global, Linda supports and guides ambitious, creative women to move in the direction of their purpose, their mission, and their dreams with powerful connections, critical support, practical tools, and valuable resources to show up, speak up, and step up in their careers and personal lives.

https://LeadHERshipGlobal.com
Facebook.com/leadhershipglobal
Twitter.com/leadhershipglob
Instagram.com/leadhershipglobal
Linkedin.com/company/leadhershipglobal

RECOGNIZE EQUALITY
BY PRECIOUS FULLER

Introduction

D o you remember the last time you connected with someone? I *mean really connected* to the point that you learned about the person's needs and were able to offer help in meaningful ways. Well, if you did, you received something in return. I'll let you determine what that was for your specific situation. The point I'm making is that you cannot help others without also helping yourself. What we put out into our human circle has a way of boomeranging back around. We are interconnected as members of this human family. So, when you invest in others, you in turn have invested in yourself. If you are adding value or making contributions in your environment, it is because someone took a chance on you or invested in you! Someone could have advocated for you without you even knowing it. You were deemed a worthy investment. When an investment is made, the return is expected to be greater than that investment. Were you worth it? Are you worth it? Here's another question: Is someone else worth your investment? If your answer is yes, what is your view of the individual that brings you to that answer? What kind of system is used to determine value?

Hierarchy

In organizations, there is a model where some people are at the top and others flow to the bottom. This pyramid is set up like a hierarchy. There is a clear distinction in the roles and perceived value of those at the top compared to those at the bottom. The organization runs when everyone knows his or her role and operates in it accordingly. If the leaders at the top, who are considered "more" valuable were there by themselves, the business would not run as well and in some cases, it wouldn't run at all. So, that pyramid would surely fall without the people who know how to do the work and then commit to doing it. Let's explore a view of equality in those systems. If we realize the importance of every role in the organization, we are aligning in understanding the value of every member of the team and each one's specific and necessary contribution. Our roles vary and so may our contributions. We can acknowledge this fact without diminishing the value of others who are equal to ourselves in our shared humanity. Let's look at this last point a few different ways.

Value vs. Contribution

First, how do you weigh value versus contribution? What's most important for an organization to receive from its stakeholders, value or contribution? **Value** is the importance, worth, or usefulness of something. (Definitions from Oxford Languages.) **Contribution** is the part played by a person in bringing about a result or helping something to advance. (Definitions from Oxford Languages.) Let's look at the question again. When looking at your team, staff, or organization, do they add value to you? Do they provide contribution? There is a way of getting both value and contribution. That comes through valuing each employee. We get the person and from the person we get the contributions. When we recognize the value of a person and invest accordingly, the individual contributions are manifested. Beyond seeing the value of our stakeholders, when they truly "feel" valued by their leaders, their contributions are multiplied, ad infinitum! Now some people may choose to value the contributions over the contributor, and they can miss out on the second point, which is investment.

Relationship Investment

We invest in what and whom we believe has value or will add value to us and our endeavors. Our main resources of time, money, and energy require investment from us if we want to maximize them. Our relationship with these resources is reflected in our investment. Our relationship and view of time determines how we use it and maximize it. Our relationship with money helps to determine the amount of it that we have and how we manage it. How we expend our energy is reflected in the activities we engage in and those we avoid so we can preserve our energy for things and people we value most. The final investment I will mention here is the one of **relationship with others**. The previous resources can be classified as either intangible, neutral, or concepts. When we deal with relationships with others however, they are animate. People are live and real. Due to being neither intangible, neutral, or concepts, our relationships with people require a different level of investment and risk. It involves risk because the results are based on more than our efforts alone. The other person's response is the other half of the equation. As we recognize the value in others, it brings that risk factor down and we become more willing to invest. We visualize the possibilities and results that can come from our relationship investment with them. People are, and always will be more valuable than things. The two categories of 1) People versus 2) Things or Concepts cannot be compared. People are human, alive. People are value. People are "worth." Things or concepts are given value by us. They are intangible and inanimate. So, to acknowledge, appreciate, and accept people and their value requires my third point for realizing man's equality and that is a Sabbath.

Sabbath

There is a familiar and modestly practiced tradition in the Christian faith of the Sabbath. The Sabbath is a weekly time of rest, reflection, and rejuvenation. This time affords the observers to rest their bodies from its toil, reflect on one's Creator and His sovereignty in their lives, and become rejuvenated through the process of rest and reflection. Sabbath observers take themselves out of the unending grind of work for rest to restore their bodies and minds. They spend time in reflection and recognize more of what they are grateful for. Part of this reflection is recognizing and appreciating others and connecting more deeply with them. The time investment from the rest and reflection results in more clarity and rejuvenation. Rejuvenation results in energy. Reflection produces clearer perspective of our inanimate resources in contrast to our relationships with people. Who are the people we love, trust, and hold most valuable? When we rest, we maximize our use of time and can be more intentional in how we use it going forward. When we take a Sabbath rest and reflect as well as rejuvenate, we can place value on people over products and concepts. By observing this time, we take ourselves out of the hustle and bustle of life long enough to intentionally appreciate what we have, who we have, and the value we place on it all. Developing this perspective on the importance of human relationships and their value to us does not come from our drive to acquire more. That would only keep us on the hamster wheel of life, going nowhere fast, as we work to attain more and are still left unsatisfied. Things do not have the ability to care about the investment we place into them. Things cannot even care about us. As inanimate or intangible objects, they simply cannot. Only people can respond to our investments and appreciate us in return. The Sabbath helps us to disengage from the routine and to recognize and appreciate the most relevant.

Conclusion

Valuing people before benefitting from their contribution, investing in quality relationships with them, and observing weekly times of rest for reflection and rejuvenation helps us operate out of an abundance mindset and not out of a scarcity mindset. We have an abundance of perspective, fulfillment, and quality of life when we recognize all that we have as opposed to what we want and feel we need. When was the last time you rested, reflected, and were rejuvenated? It's something we need regularly to help us keep first things first and value life and relationships accordingly.

In naming this chapter, "Recognize Equality," it is to reveal that the choice is ours to recognize our human equality. We are all a part of the same human family and as we treat each other with mutual respect, we are fulfilling The Golden Rule. This Golden Rule of treating others as we would want to be treated connects the humanity in us with the humanity in our fellow man and woman. The Golden Rule, shared in every religion and expressed from Christianity, Judaism, Islam, Buddhism, Confucianism, Hinduism, Sikhism, Jainism, Taoism, & Baha`'i` recognizes man's equality and his responsibility to reflect that as he would like it reflected on himself

(Oneness Great Principles Shared By All Religions, Jeffrey Moses, pp. 5-7). This level of connection is our deepest investment and develops our greatest reward, in business as well as in life. The Declaration of Independence for the United States of America records the phrase, "We hold these truths to be self-evident that all men are created equal" (1776, https://www.archives. gov). The fact that the writers of the Declaration wrote these words did not make them true. The writers merely recorded what is self-evident and had the opportunity to align with truth. They did not create it, however. Writing or speaking words does not make us believe them or live by them. Whether we believe or live by them is a choice. Truth was here long before we were and does not ask our permission to be. It simply is! All who accept and align with truth are part of a deeper and more powerful business plan, agenda, and system. We can choose whether we accept and align with truth. We cannot change, diminish, or alter whether it is truth.

Summation

Recognizing the equality of our team, staff, or organization would lead us to treat them with that knowledge and recognition. As we act on that knowledge, our beliefs are reflected through our investments. When we invest in others, we benefit also. These kinds of benefits cannot be hoarded, only shared. So, you say you want to grow your business and leave a lasting legacy? Then you need to make some intentional investments in valuing others as you value yourself.

"When people look upon others as extensions of themselves, all obstacles to fulfillment are removed—both for individuals and society. When the goals of every individual are supported by the activities of every other person, the world has the possibility to flourish in peace and prosperity. For this reason, the Golden Rule should not be thought of as a vague ideal. It is a practical principle that embodies the deepest aspirations of humanity. It serves as the basis for all that is positive and lasting in human life" (Oneness Great Principles Shared by all Religions, Jeffrey Moses, p. 4).

Wisdom Gained from the Journey to Ennoble Business

1. There is untapped talent just waiting to connect with leaders who truly value them.
2. Inclusive leadership comes from valuing others and reflecting that out.
3. Rest and reflection help us to "prioritize" so we can place value with "people and our relationships with them."
4. Great and effective leaders love people and see their inherent value.
5. As leaders value their people, the resulting contributions are limitless.

Precious Fuller is the CEO of Equanimity Partners Intl., a Human Equity Management Consulting Firm. Precious helps companies improve their workplace culture and maximize their employee potential through leadership training and retention strategies. She believes in supporting culturally competent leaders who are engaged and motivated to deliver exceptional results at every level of their organization. Precious is an expert in Employee Training & Retention, Diversity & Inclusion in the Workplace, and Leadership Development. She has a master's degree in Teaching and work experience in education as well as inside a national non-profit organization environment.

Precious is a leading edge socialpreneur who is passionate about enhancing the 'human condition.' She does this through her coaching, consulting, and speaking. Her coaching and consulting revolve around diversity, equity, & inclusion with her speaking being centered in human rights. Precious promotes the equality and fair treatment of humanity with special emphasis on racial equity. She works with executives, leaders & professionals, individually and in group settings using one-to-one and group coaching formats for leadership development and personal development. Precious is an accomplished professional of over 20 years with experience in education, life-skills training, diversity, equity & inclusion, human relations, and strategic planning. In her role of human equity management, Precious works to establish diverse and inclusive cultures in support of all humanity.

Precious.fuller@equanimitypartnersintl.com
318-459-8817
www.EquanimityPartnersIntl.com
https://www.linkedin.com/in/preciousfuller-diversity-equity-inclusion
-specialist

HIDDEN POTENTIAL
BY NERMINE ZAKHARY

Parable of the Talents

Growing up, my favorite Bible story was the Parable of the Talents (Matthew 25:14-30). The Master gave one servant five talents, another servant two talents and a third servant one talent. The one who had the five produced five more. The one who had two produced two more. The one who had one talent buried it in the ground. When the Master returned, he rewarded the servants who doubled what they had received, saying, "Well done, good and faithful servant. Enter into the joy of your Lord." He condemned the servant who buried his one talent, calling him wicked and lazy and took that one talent away.

The message? God makes it clear that He expects us to use the talents He has given us, and not just to use them, but to double what we've received! This led me to wonder as I was growing up, *How do I know what my talents are?*

Signs of My Personality

I had always been fascinated with the amazing things people can do. I was curious about their interests, their talents, and what led them to pursue certain fields or activities, and I have fond memories of exchanging letters with my aunts and uncles in Egypt, concentrating on their professions or unique interests. I gravitated toward young adults in our travels and chatted with them about what they loved to do and how they wanted to impact the world.

By college, I thought I knew *my* answer. In the Egyptian culture, education and achievement are prized. In my senior year of high school, I was already making the grade, student council president, number 1 in my class. I loved biology and chemistry and knew I wanted to help people. I was going to follow in my father's footsteps and become a doctor. Everyone around me fed this expectation. I received awards and scholarships and heard repeatedly, "Nermine is going into the medical field . . ."

Then reality took hold. During my freshman year, I failed my first biology exam. It was quite a shock to my system. Although I managed to recover and did well enough to pass my next exam, this failure shook me up enough to ask, *Is this what I really want? Do I love it enough to work this hard for the next 8 years of my life?* That question put me in a spiral. I started to explore other fields: economics, sociology . . . *nothing* was *satisfying*. I ended up graduating with a B.A. in biology, basically an unusable, general science degree, and never did apply for medical school.

This experience colored my life for the next 20 years. I felt like a failure. I kept wondering who I was, what happened to me, what was wrong with me. Ultimately, after some key events in my life, I felt moved to finally go back to school and pursue my master's degree, which took me to Xerox.

Then one afternoon I learned of a workshop called "Discover Your Strengths" and so intrigued, I immediately signed up. We were instructed to take the StrengthsFinder 2.0 assessment to prepare, and . . . I was disappointed with the results! My top five strengths included a lot of relationship words, and they seemed fluffy to me. My first reaction was that this was just another silly personality test.

But my feelings soon changed. In one of the exercises, we were asked to jot down recent activities that we looked forward to, enjoyed doing, and that made us feel strong. We were asked to share our thoughts, along with our StrengthsFinder Top 5 talent themes, with a partner. I can't remember this gentleman's name or what he looks like. All I remember is how I felt during our conversation. As I was sharing my enjoyable, strong moments, he was pointing at my strengths. "Nermine, you were using this one. Nermine, you were using that one," he kept telling me. And, oh, my goodness! I realized he was on to something as I began to understand that when I'm using my strengths, I feel happy. When I'm using my strengths, I'm doing something useful and helpful. It hit me like a ton of bricks!

In that moment, I realized that I had spent the bulk of my adult life trying to live up to someone else's (perceived) expectations, and never quite meeting them. I compared myself to someone else and thought, *Why can't I be like them? Why can't I do what she does?* And never, ever feeling good enough.

For the first time in my adult life, it was okay to just be Me. My world shifted.

I didn't know I had a calling.

I couldn't stop thinking about strengths, talking about strengths. I knew this was where I wanted to be. This is where *my* talents were, and I wanted to double them. As soon as I got my hands on coaching materials, I felt a palpable excitement! I invited anyone who was willing to engage in a practice coaching session. When my manager encouraged me to deliver a workshop for our team, for as far-removed from public speaking as I was by this time in my career, I jumped at the opportunity! Bravery fueled by sheer passion.

As I sought out training and certification, I began to delve deeper. It is one thing to know your strengths, but I soon realized the power comes from knowing what to *do* with them. That's when I happened on Strengths Strategy, now People Acuity, a company that talked about the "application of strengths." Founder DeAnna Murphy was a Gallup Strengths Coach and Franklin Covey Facilitator. She had the same realization when working with her strengths coaching clients. This led her to merge the concepts of these two brilliant methodologies into the Strategic Interdependence Model® to help us *apply* our strengths and accelerate our performance, energy, and relationships.[7] When DeAnna and I met, she was

---

[7]   DeAnna Murphy, Lisa Gregory, Steve Jeffs (2018). Shift Up! Strengths Strategies for Optimal Living. https://www.amazon.com/dp/B078T4MCD3

conducting a pilot of the certification program she had developed for this new model. I was honored to join her first official cohort, January 2014.

Achieving My Certification: God Inspired Moment

If you had told me back in high school or college or early in my career that I would be a life coach one day, I would never have believed you. Looking back, however, it makes so much sense. I've always been drawn to finding out what motivates people, and what drives them to move in different directions. I enjoy helping them uncover truths that can help them move forward.

The evening after my final oral evaluation for my Strengths Strategy Coaching Certification, I vividly remember sitting at the dinner table, feeling numb, exhausted, and elated all at the same time. I reflected on the previous two years. **It was as if God had been preparing me my whole life for this moment.** There were so many signs: the contrast between my successes in high school and failures in college, the journey through my master's degree, and my arrival at Xerox, where I had been in the right place at the right time and learned about StrengthsFinder.

I was filled with emotion and kept thinking, *If God brought me on this journey to actually becoming a Strengths coach, then someone out there must need this.*

Why do I need an assessment?

Just because our strengths are innate, that doesn't mean we can see them. They are simply how we operate, see the world, interact with others, and make decisions.[8] We don't see them as anything special. It's just who we are. They come with us everywhere we go. In fact, because they happen so naturally, we might wonder why others in our circles can't do what we do or see things the way we see them. We often get annoyed.[9]

---

[8]   Marcus Buckingham & Donald O. Clifton, Ph.D. (2001). *Now, Discover Your Strengths.* https://www.amazon.com/Discover-Your-Strengths-Marcus-Buckingham/dp/0743201140
[9]   DeAnna Murphy, Lisa Gregory, Steve Jeffs (2018). *Shift Up! Strengths Strategies for Optimal Living.* https://www.amazon.com/dp/B078T4MCD3

That's why we need an external resource, someone or something outside of ourselves to help reveal them, so we *can* see them, recognize them, speak to them, and use them more purposefully. This has become my mission—to help people *see* their Strengths and own their value, so they can go "double the talents they've been given."

Importance of Strengths-building versus Weakness-fixing

We live in a deficit-thinking society. We are quick to attempt to fix our flaws—what's wrong with us. We tend to look for the lessons learned before we discuss what went well. We don't take time to celebrate what we did accomplish. This is often the way we approach ourselves, our colleagues, and our children. I've heard Marcus Buckingham share on multiple occasions the results of a research study that posed this question to parents: "When your child comes home with an A in English, an A in social studies, a C in biology, and an F in algebra, where will you spend most of your time?" Among the participants, 77% said, "The F in algebra."

Think about this. What is in store for this child who has little acknowledgement of the As in English and social studies! That child will see the Fs and gloss over the As.[10]

As DeAnna is fond of saying, "Whichever you *see*, that's where you'll *be*." In other words, you can choose to look at your deficits and focus on what you need to fix in your life. Or, you can choose to look at your gifts, where you find energy and perform well. The beauty is that when you start to recognize your strengths, it's natural to become curious about other people's strengths! What a gift! What a blessing to our relationships (especially with those we tend to avoid because we "clash")![11]

As we uncover talents we may not have been able to see, the journey takes on a different quality. We begin to accept what we may have rejected about ourselves and about others in the past. Our view shifts, and we notice the value other people bring to our lives. Our gratitude grows. What a healing concept.

---

[10] Ibid.
[11] Ibid.

Where to Start!

With or without an official strengths profile, you can begin to discover your strengths and help others do the same. Start by asking yourself:

- What do I do well?

- Are there phrases or compliments I hear often?

Buckingham provides additional questions to ask: What activities are you naturally drawn to? Where does learning come easily? When do you feel deep satisfaction and contentment? How about when you experience "flow," so engrossed in an activity that you lose all track of time? And finally, what about those glimpses of excellence, when you look back and say, "Wow—I did that!"[12]

You are so Special!

I want to leave you with this. Did you know that each person has 8-10 strengths that they play to strongly by the time they're an adult? And the chances you will find someone with the same top 10 StrengthsFinder results (in the same order) as you, are *1 in 467 trillion*??!!![13] That's how unique and special you are! You have something only *you* can contribute to our world. Let's figure out what that is so you can go do it on purpose—and make your precious mark on our world!

How I Help

Today I use my coaching tools to help people who have a team they absolutely adore but feel may be under-utilized. They're concerned about how to leverage that fabulous potential and want to maximize happiness and productivity, to create a cohesive environment where employee and organization can thrive together.

---

[12] Marcus Buckingham & Donald O. Clifton, Ph.D. (2001). *Now, Discover Your Strengths.* https://www.amazon.com/Discover-Your-Strengths-Marcus-Buckingham/dp/0743201140
[13] DeAnna Murphy, Lisa Gregory, Steve Jeffs (2018). *Shift Up! Strengths Strategies for Optimal Living.* https://www.amazon.com/dp/B078T4MCD3

"Don't over-improve your weaknesses. If you're not good at something, work on it until it no longer prevents your progress, but the bulk of your time is better spent maximizing your strengths."[14]
—James Clear

Wisdom Gained from the Journey to Ennoble Business

Shifting your focus to strengths-building instead of weakness-fixing

1. Builds up your confidence as a leader,
2. Communicates appreciation and caring to your team,
3. Impacts your bottom line because your people only want to bring you their best!

Nermine Zakhary is a Certified People Acuity Coach™ & Positive Intelligence (PQ) Coach, specializing in helping others strategically apply their strengths to accelerate their performance, energy, relationships, and results.

As a PQ Coach, Nermine adds the important layer of helping clients grow their mental fitness (the capacity to handle life's challenges with a positive mindset), the next step in ensuring lifelong application of strengths.

Nermine coaches individuals and small groups. She also facilitates workshops to teach strengths strategies to clients so they can define their optimal zones—and thrive there.

Nermine comes to Strengths & PQ coaching with 15+ years of experience in the training industry at Highland Hospital and Xerox Corporation. She holds a master's degree in Education, specializing in Instructional Design for Online Learning.

---

[14]   James Clear (2021). "3-2-1: Ending the year on a high note, maximizing your strength, and taking responsibility." https://jamesclear.com/3-2-1/december-23-2021

I spent most of my adolescent and young adult years attempting to live up to the expectations of others. I always found myself in comparison-mode, feeling 'not good enough,' i.e.: stuck in weakness-fixing. When I came upon the CliftonStrengths assessment (formerly known as StrengthsFinder 2.0), I began to understand how I'm wired and that when I use my talents, I offer something valuable. My world shifted!

I've been on a mission ever since, to foster 'strengths-based' thinking everywhere I go and with everyone I meet. I want others to live their best lives, armed with a full knowledge of their strengths.

My wish for you is that you will . . .

Rise to your Strengths-Edge—Because it's in You!

Nermine

Email Address: nermine@strengths-edge.com
Phone Number: 585.687.8704
Website: www.Strengths-Edge.com
Facebook page(s): http://www.facebook.com/strengthsedge
LinkedIn Page: https://www.linkedin.com/in/nerminezakhary/

PART TWO

Ignite the Sense of Purpose

HINDSIGHT 2020:
LIBERATING THE
SUBLIMINAL POTENTIAL
BY NANDINI MENON, MD

The year 2020 was supposed to be the year of the Eye-care Professionals in the United States. Then, the pandemic hit . . . and that brilliant play on the 20/20 vision ad campaigns and slogans was thrown to the wayside all over the US. For the first time, even the healthcare industry shut down and I, like the rest of the world, had the time for introspection and self-realization to envision what my future should look like.

I had spent the past 11 years trying to come to terms with balancing the dualism of an altruistic personality with the capitalism of being a physician in the United States. In hindsight, when I finally admitted I needed help, I realize now I was looking for answers to the wrong problem. I didn't realize I was trying so hard to fit the mold of the *American Dream*, I had lost sight of who I was and what I believed in.

In 2020, I was in the middle of a partnership negotiation and I found myself finally facing my nemesis—accounting—and trying to understand the finances of a business. I enrolled in a training program and started the course with the intent of learning about running a business, specifically about its finances and the basics of accounting. What I got was far more valuable and liberating.

Most physicians want nothing to do with the business and the administrative side of medicine, and I was no different. Knowing this about myself, I embarked on my budding medical career, with my ideal job, as an employee physician in the government service in Malaysia. As life evolved, I followed my heart and moved continents for the man I love. So, the year 2002 found me in the country that is the beacon of capitalism and individualism, trying to live the *American Dream*. Against all odds and naysayers, I got back into one of the most coveted of residencies in the US, for Ophthalmology. In 2009, still with no interest in the administrative and financial side of medicine, I joined a private practice that I thought would allow me to continue to concentrate on patient care.

As I continued to work, I quickly realized that healthcare is run like a business, with profit and loss being judged in terms of money revenue and shareholder happiness. For someone with a naïve and idealistic view of the medical profession, it has been very difficult for me to come to terms with the monetizing of the profession. My professional discontent fed into personal discontent.

In my 4th or 5th year of practice in the US, I found myself misunderstood and unable to communicate simple requests. My inner circle were pointing to communication skills as the problem. As someone who was always complimented for her great communication skills and being a people's person, this was hard to accept and I perceived it as criticism. This fed my insecurities and the narrative that I was not given the same respect as my male colleagues. It took another two years before I admitted to myself I had to change and try to rectify the problem on my own. Over the next few years, the negative self-talk and miscommunication continued, and slowly trickled into all facets of my life, including my personal relationships. My personal and work life fell apart. Overwhelmed, I was no longer the confident, calm, and collected professional or person and finally decided to seek help.

Medical school excels in teaching the art and science of practicing medicine, but fails to addresses managing the medical practice. No thought is given to building, running, and sustaining a business, or of leading and communicating with emotional intelligence. We are honed and given the tools to treat ills of the human body, its physical, emotional, and mental wellbeing, but not the tools or skills to address the human *inside* our body. On the contrary, we are taught to be "unemotional" and to ignore or suppress our own feelings. Held to a higher standard of emotional, physical, and mental endurance, we are expected to function at 110%, especially when sleep deprived and with physical exhaustion.

Over the past decade, the wheels of the oligarchy are changing, although slowly. The rules about work hour limits and mandatory time off after calls have addressed physical and mental fatigue during training.[15] Emotional fatigue and burnout of physicians is the new frontier. Enhancing the emotional coefficient opens the floodgates to compassion, empathy, and overall improvement of life satisfaction scores for staff, patients, and physicians alike. The biggest elephant in the room to address this is improving the communication and leadership skills of a physician.

Effective communication in a leadership role is not barking out an order. It's getting your team to work as a cohesive unit. As physicians, we spend the majority of our lives working with people who do not have the specialized knowledge or the wherewithal to understand the circuits of a physician's brain, especially during medical emergencies, when time is of the essence. Trust helps someone to execute your directive, even though they don't necessarily understand the why. The result is that the staff and management feel vested in the patient care process and their job satisfaction is improved. This human skill helps the office run smoothly, without being labelled rude, condescending or "bossy" and leads to better employee retention. This skill inherently requires improving emotional intelligence and building trust. It may even convince patients to take ownership of healthy lifestyle changes that hopefully lead to better adherence to treatment and improved patient satisfaction—ultimately resulting in a more content and well-balanced doctor, who can concentrate on what they love doing: treating the human condition.

The lessons life teaches us aren't always the ones we set out to learn. The training program I took was to learn the basics of finance; instead, it gave me very different and life-changing lessons about myself. My self-confidence was at an all-time low. I had to face and work through difficult conversations in multiple personal relationships. As I learnt about the different ways people communicate based on an individual's gender, cultural, generational, and geographical influences, it dawned on me that I didn't suddenly lose my

---

[15] 2014 Oct;33(10):1832-40. doi: 10.1377/hlthaff.2014.0318. PMID: 25288430; PMCID: PMC4269477

communication skills. I was communicating as an East Asian, in a Western Anglo-Saxon US culture. This was truly the "aha!" moment, for it opened my mind's eye and energized me. There was nothing wrong with me!

I just needed to learn to communicate in a different cultural environment. Recognizing the nuances of the way people communicate with me and understanding how to communicate with them was just the start. The improved skills I acquired made me a better leader professionally, and also helped my personal relationships. Recognizing subconscious biases (triggers) in ourselves and the people closest to us helps us resolve conflicts and come to decisions without hurtful arguments and resentment, because in these situations, reactions are emotional and words are taken too personally. The personality exercise integrated into the program I took with *Johari Window* and using the "*5 Whys*" gave me an understanding of myself, and specifically, about my weaknesses, my triggers, and my blind spots. The recognition and control I got over subconscious biases and negative emotions was simultaneously liberating and empowering. These relatively simple exercises helped turn my triggers into my "*Nijavirya.*"

Nijavirya is the Sanskrit word for innate strength.[16] *Nija* means self / own.[17] *Virya* is strength or potency.[18] In other words, your untapped or subliminal potential—what the western world calls your superpower. What makes you tick? That which makes you whole. It is the essence of who we are as humans. Once you embrace it and resolve to make choices around it, you automatically thrive. It's a natural way to prevent burnout, and increase your happiness score (aka life satisfaction) in any job or crossroad in life.

Negotiations permeate every aspect of all our lives, as parents, friends, coworkers, leaders, and with our life partners. Being aware and managing triggers turns them into subliminal strengths as communicator for any situation in life where two or more parties have to come to agreement. In essence, a better negotiator. Communication is an essential skill for a productive dialogue; therefore, being effective at it puts you in a position of strength during negotiation, including an employment contract, a business contract, or an informal contract (like with patients or loved ones about their health).

---

[16] Srimad Bhagavad Geeta 1.10.22
[17] https://www.wisdomlib.org/definition/nija
[18] https://www.wisdomlib.org/definition/virya

I don't regret the past 25 years that brought me to this moment, if it helps the next generation learn the important role these human skills play in their lives sooner. Imparting this knowledge to young adults in any field, especially healthcare, will give them a head start. Learning these skills as students or young professionals in the dawn of their careers will help them find the right position with the right work culture sooner. Figuring out what we are good at and learning to overcome what we are afraid of helps us find our Nijavirya. Knowing what gives us joy and what doesn't, even in mundane activities, plays a pivotal role in job and life satisfaction. Navigating this early helps us to recognize strengths and weaknesses in ourselves and in others. Practicing this skill gives us the courage to delegate the right tasks to the right people, ultimately surrounding ourselves with people who compliment our weaknesses and enhance our strengths, making a wholesome team around a vision for our lives. This is how we continue to have long and happy careers, even as physicians, with an active and well-balanced life. These lessons transcend the field of medicine, and are applicable to any individual, business, or organization. **Liberate and harness the subliminal potential from within, and you will thrive.** When you thrive, your organization thrives and so do the people around you. Together, we can all thrive.

The medical profession has to accept that we run a business. We are in the business of improving the human condition. Therefore, we have to start incorporating some basic finance and management skills to negotiate, delegate, and improve the running of our business. It's hard enough keeping up with medical innovation. Most of us don't have time to sign up for an MBA or figure out the nuances of keeping employees happy. Yet we are all the CEO and CFO of our own lives and definitely part of the C-suite. We need to start teaching the skills required to be a confident or effective part of the conversation that impacts the well-being of the individuals with whom we spend the most time in our lives, including ourselves. Medical training has to evolve and meet the changing times in the practice of medicine; otherwise, we are constantly going to be our own worst enemy.

This pandemic has shown that burnout is rampant in every sector of humanity. From parenting, to the grocery workers, from our toddlers to the teens, our workload is harder, and our effects of stressors on our psyche have worsened. For physicians as well, our self-care and burnout prevention are in the forefront of our minds. The need for physicians in the US and around the world is going to skyrocket, especially in these times. Building emotional intelligence, mindful communication, and leadership skills into medical school and resident teaching curriculum will improve physician life satisfaction alongside staff and patient satisfaction.

In this era of social media and the internet, globalization affects all of us. Our collective future is intertwined, be it personal or professional. Chances are to set up businesses and to create coalitions and partnerships (both in our personal and professional lives) will require interaction with people of different cultures, countries, and communication styles. It is inevitable that all of us will need to learn to communicate and navigate emotions both on a personal and professional level with people of varied cultures. Being open to understanding the disconnect between who we project ourselves to be, vs how we are perceived, makes us stronger and better versions of ourselves. It helps us realize our *nijavirya*.

Wisdom Gained from the Journey to Ennoble Business

1. **Be open to change.** There are no "mistakes or bad decision," just opportunities to take stock and rethink the path to success
2. **Listen without bias.** "Criticism" of you or your idea, is about unconscious biases and fears, not a personal attack.
3. **Face fears head on.** Focus on solutions to generate a positive internal narrative and outlook to life.

Nandini Menon, MD took a leap of faith and moved to Chicago in the United States of America at the age of 29, after a semi-traditional arranged marriage to her husband Gopi. She never gave up on her dream job of being an Eye Surgeon. Her resilience, grace, and personality broke the barriers and biases one at a time, and she got back into Ophthalmology to complete her training at Northwestern University.

Born in the town of Johor Bahru located at the southern tip of Malaysia, her formative years were spent in an idyllic setting, surrounded by open spaces and the sweet, nutty smell of palm oil. Though her early education was split between Malaysia and Singapore, she maintained strong roots to her South Asian heritage thanks to many school holidays spent with her grandparents at her ancestral home in Kerala, India. Living in India for her medical training at Kasturba Medical College in Manipal, and exposure to different communities as a young professional, in Malaysia, India, and the USA helped her understand and take pride in her nomadic cultural identity.

Dr. Menon continues to practice Ophthalmology in Albuquerque, New Mexico, USA where she lives with her husband. The varied and global exposure has made her aware of inherent social and subconscious biases in every society and aspects of daily life. She is especially interested in helping people, especially in healthcare, recognize and use this knowledge to enhance the quality of their lives, and improve their overall health and satisfaction.

Email: menonn13@gmail.com
Facebook: https://www.facebook.com/menonn13
Instagram: dr.n.menon
LinkedIn: www.linkedin.com/in/nandini-menon-md-8b55a112

BECOMING VISABLE
BY MARQUESE MARTIN-HAYES

According to the Glenn Lois Group's 2013 study, "Less than 15% of people have truly defined their personal brand and less than 5% are living it consistently at work." (https://www.forbes.com/sites/glennllopis/2013/04/08/personal-branding-is-a-leadership-requirement-not-a-self-promotion-campaign/). This means that 95% of us are frauds and phony for the majority of our day.

When we don't know who we are, we become whatever works to get ahead. Actually, I mean we only survive if all things in life work to our benefit.

Do yourself a favor right now. Think about the people you work with. This means 9.5 out of your ten friends in your group are pretending to be happy. Literally, 95 out of 100 people you know are doing whatever it takes to get by.

What happened?

Ground Zero Has Potential

Imagine growing up and spending your entire life *not knowing who you are.* What would that feel like? How would you make decisions? The Tough Fact is many of us still don't. Of course, I had no idea then, but it is where my company, The Vissable Group Inc. began to germinate within me. Growing up, I felt alone even though I was surrounded by a loving community. Even though I had a wonderful community, there seemed to be a disconnect. How? Well, as fate would have it, my parents were teenagers when they conceived me. So naturally, it was difficult for them to know what to do with me. They still needed and wanted to go out, go to high school, look good, have fun, and learn about life, as teenagers. They wanted to know who they were too!

In a basic sense, I was raised with my parents. They were two kids who after a wild night were stuck trying to figure out what to do with this infant. And to sweeten the deal, they did not continue seeing one another and chose to do life independently. No matter how amazing the family and community were, the feeling of not knowing who I was and internal inadequacy was my accepted reality. I mean, they were teenagers, not parents.

Being the only child between my teenage parents, I developed a reality that governed my life. It included some basic idea that I was in this world alone and that I was a bother to my grandparents, aunts, and uncles. Definitely, to my parents. Where was my mom? Why wasn't my dad fighting to take me in and raise me? It seemed the only thing that mattered was doing right by God, the church, and the community. For me, all those things culminated into, *"I'm not good enough and I need to perform in order to be noticed or accepted."*

"Doing right" and "pleasing others" became my badge of honor and passion. If only I could just "stay out of trouble." Clearly, I wasn't successful, I'm human, but it didn't stop the internal journey of pursuing this deep need to feel as I now see it . . . Loved.

Those were my keys to winning in life!

Those keys also became my prison. I conformed to be accepted. I walked away from *me*, the unique being *me*. For decades I had no clue what my desires were, what I preferred. What was the version of life that I wanted to live? I had accepted the simple lie of just doing right and the rest will come to you. That was my personal brand, doing what everyone else thought I should do.

I was a ninety-five percenter.

I'm sure your version of life matches mine or at least you've felt similar feelings. It's common. Common to be a ninety-five percenter. Much like computers, whatever the software allows us to do, we do—not realizing that we could rewrite the code and create our own software, or even that there are alternatives available. Instead, we simply work within the confines of the computer we have, complain about the problems, and wait for an upgrade.

Why Do I Do What I Do?

Have you ever wondered why you live where you live, work where you work, wear the types of clothing you wear, and talk about the things you mostly talk about? It's essentially blind patriotism. I think don Miguel Ruiz said it best in his book *The Four Agreements*, summarized as, ". . . you don't believe what you believe. You believe what you've been given, without the option of exposure to something contrary equally long. At least then you could make a full comparison and freely choose."

This has become the way of the ninety-five percenters.

Take what you can get. Because at least you have something and hey, retirement is coming. Are you truly fulfilled? What would your life look like if you were actually living your dreams? Not the dreams that you've altered for "reality." Your *dreams*. The ones you had as a youth about what you could become, what you would like to have, about who you'd like to be.

I'm not suggesting that you stop everything, abandon your responsibilities, and give up the things you have. I'm simply asking, *How did you get here?*

Chaos Breeds Possibility

Fortunately for me, my parents' very different lifestyles gave me clips, moments, and glimpses of possibility. My mother joined the army and took us to Germany for a few years and back to the Pacific Northwest, Washington State. It was in those spaces, that I had my worldview blown and reshaped.

I went to school with the world. I was beautifully bombarded with culture, expressions, insights, and value from people who didn't look like me. It was without a doubt one of the most fascinating gifts ever.

My father, on the other hand, went into network marketing and personal development. It taught me that anything was literally possible, even though I hadn't understood it. I remember being forced to listen to cassette tapes of the stories of common folk, describing many of their challenges, seemingly failures, and mental anguish they had experienced while pursuing their dreams. Beautifully, every cassette ended with the people having either recently crossed a milestone or having fully manifested their dreams. They'd arrived at some level of success and felt joy and self-accomplishment that exceeded their dreams and now they wanted to help others too! Those cassette tapes became my fairytales. Unknowingly, also my foundation.

Identify the Moments

All of us have had moments. Moments where the lights of possibility came on. Moments where we could imagine. Moments where our minds would be blown. It's those seeds that hopefully germinate and grow within us all.

Living a life of self-inflicted abandonment of my emotions and feelings for the sake of others' feelings and approval created an internal longing—a longing to see *what if*. What if people could be accepted for who they were? Have you ever heard the phrase, you can't judge a book by its cover? That became my life experience. While I lived feeling like not enough, and afraid to fully self-express, I noticed it within others and wanted them to "have their dreams" at all costs. So even though I felt like I couldn't necessarily have mine, I would try to help others identify a way to have their fulfillment, just like the people on the recordings. I decided that would be my life mission: empower others to see how amazing they already are, by removing the barriers mentally, physically, and emotionally. I'd figured that if more people could discover themselves, then the world would be a better place. People would be happier, and we would have a lot more love flowing in our homes, communities, and the planet.

We're Better Together

My first attempt at unifying and expanding the concept of us all having value began at The Marketplace. It was a uniquely designed conversation space that brought people from all races, nationalities, religious beliefs, sexual preferences, and more. And it was a success!!! We would gather weekly in Chicago around simple universal-yet-potentially-controversial ideas and discuss our individual experiences and expressions in a safe place among "others." It was there that we discovered much of what we believed was given to us versus derived from our own experience, intellect, and research. We found that we have far more in common than we are different and that our differences were our gifts to one another.

The Marketplace bred an acceptance atmosphere and stimulated unlikely, and now lifelong, relationships—all centered around being seen, heard, and challenged. As a result, we were all better humans in every area of our lives.

Imagine if we truly saw each other for who we are, not what we do.

Enter The Vissable Group. Imagine waking up and living out the things that give you the most joy. Not happiness which can change from moment to moment, but pure internal joy. That begins with self-discovery and awareness. Although it is foreign to many of us, imagine if you earned your living from the expression of who you are versus what you have learned to be and do?

What would you do for work? Who would you work for?

The ongoing quest to help others be seen, heard, and valued from my own need growing up has now come together for the employer and employee. The idea of being a five percenter is over. We can live in a world where our own uniqueness has a chance to breathe. Vissable is the gateway to not only finding the right person, but also the right representative for companies. For the individual, they are the foundation of discovery for oneself in the context of their contribution to the planet through their work.

Choose to be seen and heard from your deepest expressions. You matter. Your gifts matter. You might be the difference. It's time to take off your façade and live!

Here are some things that you can do to discover Who You Are.

- Take some time for Self-Awareness. These questions can begin the journey:
  - If time and money were not a concern, what would you do for work?
  - If you could be anywhere in the world, where would you be and why?
  - What would you do for free?
  - What are one or two things that bother you the most in life? With the world, planet, human experience?
  - What do you have, know, or burns inside of you to do about it from the space of love?
- Why do you believe what you believe? Read don Miguel Ruiz's book *The Four Agreements* after you've answered that question, then ask yourself again.
- Dr. Myles Monroe once said that the goal is not to die old, but rather to die empty. Empty because you gave every gift and talent you have to the world. What do you want to be known for by your great grandchildren? Your community? Your country? The world?

As you answer those key internal questions, you'll begin to discover *you*. The real you, not your job, title, or profession. The part of you that the world actually needs, that you won't compromise ever again.

Wisdom Gained from the Journey to Ennoble Business

1. **Get Familiar with YOU:** likes, dislikes, preferences, shadow sides—Who you are?
2. **Do A Brain Discovery Dump of YOU and YOUR DESIRES—Let Go!** Write down everything that brings the best version of you to light.
3. **Start Today**—Implement, by creating space in your schedule to spend time devoted to YOU.

Being seen and heard are your most valuable contributions to this life. We need you. Your uniqueness matters! It's time to move beyond existing and start living! Be Vissable!

Marquese Martin-Hayes is a man on a mission to empower others to discover how amazing they already are by removing the barriers that get in the way of their lives. Some of those barriers are mental, physical, and emotional, or any variable combination. He's been a student of Human Performance and Happiness for over 35 years.

Groomed as a military child on one end and personal development on the other, he's a well-rounded communicator. As a former ultra-marathoner, he has incorporated the discipline of the body, mind, and spirit in his communication. He knows the human spirit is capable of accomplishing at any age.

Marquese is the founder of The Vissable Group Inc. a company that helps people be seen and heard beyond their resume and then partner them with companies looking for not only the right person but the right representative. He's the co-founder of a couple of different wellness companies. He dabbles in other quality living ideas. His latest endeavors include a sequel to his book *Monday Again?!*, another book on social exchange, his signature Wellness weight loss seminar "15lbs in 30 days," twitter tags #DaddyDialogs and #BeYourIcon.

Marquese will tell you that your perspective will determine your actions because your beliefs dictate your reality. He is dedicated to helping you develop the Proper Perspective so that You can materialize the Dream within and reap the rewards of being who you really are, TODAY!

IG: https://www.instagram.com/themarquese/
Twitter: https://twitter.com/themarquese
LinkedIn: https://www.linkedin.com/in/marquese/
YouTube: https://www.youtube.com/c/MarqueseMartinHayes
Facebook: https://www.fb.com/theMarquese
www.Vissable.com

JOINING THE DOTS BACKWARD
TO MOVE FORWARD
BY MARY VAZ

"Why are you not finishing up your dinner? There are children starving to death," I can hear my mum saying to my sister, who was pushing aside the greens on her plate. "Behave yourself. Be a good girl. Don't ask for anything," Mum whispered into my ear as she dressed me when I was seven in preparing for an afternoon outing with my aunt. Born as the eldest daughter in Penang to a Chinese mother and a Eurasian father, my mixed parentage has me classified as 'others' in Malaysia and considered a woman of color in Australia.

I was a minority in my country of origin, and now a minority in Australia, my home for the last 17 years. Accustomed to being a minority, working harder to be seen and earning the right to be accepted in environments in which I am different from the dominant group has been my way of life.

Looking Back

My mother always told stories about money that was part of her family's identity. She spoke with pride about how her father, a migrant from mainland China made his fortune from slaving away as a mining coolie in Ipoh to becoming a philanthropist who appreciated his cultural roots after settling down in his adopted homeland. Sadness lingered whenever she spoke about patrilineal inheritance customs practiced by her father, where only male children can inherit. She had never said it, but I wondered if she ever felt left out of her prosperous destiny. My father, son of an educator, on the other hand, avoided any talks about money. It made him uncomfortable. He felt secure and was contented earning a salary as a clerical public servant to feed his wife and four daughters.

When growing up, I was aware of the opposing stance my parents had on money—Mother with a scarcity mindset (we don't have enough) and father an advocate of living a simple life (we have enough to get by). We may not have been rich, but we were okay. My father retired when I was 15 and my youngest sister was 3. Overnight, the family income was halved. My father did not take on further employment to supplement the family income. Mother's anxiety over financial insecurity went on overdrive. Talks of not having enough, comparing the family's lack of resources with other families became part of daily conversations.

My upbringing got my childhood good-girl brain going: *I better be gainfully employed and be financially healthy when I grow up so that I can contribute to the financial wellbeing of my family to feel safe and secure.* Experiencing subtle and direct pressures to change the course of the family's financial future became wired in my upbringing. Raised wearing hand-me-downs and at the receiving end of constant reminders of how lucky we were to have a roof over our heads taught me early in life to be grateful and see the positive in life even in face of adversity. Looking back, my parents imparted the values of being grateful for the small things, big things and everything in between. Becoming a good daughter became my life's goal.

Modeling Behavior I Experienced

Since I graduated from university, I was determined to be gainfully employed, living up to my childhood aspiration. Subscribing to the mantra of working hard and playing by the rules became my motivation to keep going in the career I started. Helping with the family's financial needs started with my first pay cheque. As financial standing improved for my family, I found myself getting caught up in comparing myself using other metrics: job title, income level, paper qualifications, and other worldly successes. I adopted other people's metrics of success. Subconsciously, the concept of a good daughter morphed into the myth of a good girl (i.e., women must behave themselves and play by the rules to win in the workplace). I was guided by people-pleasing tendencies, the perceptions of what I should do and how I should behave.

Emigrating to Sydney, Australia in my late thirties and graduating from business school at 42, hitting this milestone after juggling both full-time employment whilst studying part-time was a turning point. By then, I had worked for the same global corporation across two countries and had been married to my soul mate, JR, a medical professional, for 16 years. JR was studying for his PhD full time for the initial 4 years when we arrived in Australia. Upon his graduation, he accepted a new role in a medical practice in a different state in Australia, and we relocated. The change eventually led me to step outside my comfort zone by testing my employability with other organizations. For the next 10 years, I went on to share and grow my expertise in human resources management for multiple organizations. Often, I was a minority in male-dominant environments, and frequently the only woman of color at meetings.

Using the metaphor of a quilt to represent my career over the last 10 years, my working life was starting to look and feel like a quilt patched with different materials. Some parts are wool; other parts are cashmere, denim, flannelette, fleece, cotton, linen, jersey, polyester, and many more. Some parts were smooth and comforting to feel, but significant patches were itchy to touch.

Embracing the Shift

When I was promoted to be a Director of Human Resources in a company experiencing tremendous growth, I was elated. I felt I had "arrived." I have achieved society's measure of success—a big title and my seat at the table in a land further away from my country of origin, despite being a minority. I was ever so willing to give my all regardless of the work environment I was part of. However, the incongruence in my head, heart, and gut started to weigh heavily on me. I found I was only good when I was making someone else's life easier.

When I challenged the status quo, or questioned, I was told I was too much of this or too much of that. A shift within was rising from these difficulties. A form of dormant energy was wanting to take over. Whispers of, *Stop pleasing, take a stand.* My good-girl myth was starting to wane. I was beginning to stop living my life out of fear—fear of letting others down, fear of rejection, and fear of the unknown. It dawned on me that a title is not a superpower. Getting promoted won't turn me into a superhero. A new title did not increase my ability to create impact. Unbeknownst to me, I had landed myself in the perfect, painful storm. The voice was screaming, *Enough is enough!* There was tension in the air. The dormant energy was germinating, pushing its way to subconsciousness, making the perfect storm unbearable. Along came chronic fatigue, and insomnia. The fatigue and stress I was experiencing repeated day after day without adequate opportunities to replenish and recover. During this time, some big questions floated to the surface: *What the heck am I doing? Do I want to continue down this path of self-destruction? How do I want to live out my life?*

Then burnout hit. I did not see that coming. It dawned on me that I had been running empty for some time. For several months, I was truly lost. I was confused and directionless. Recovering from burnout took time. I absorbed any self-help materials I could reach out to. After a while, I felt it was necessary to move beyond books, podcasts, and personal development programs. Going through change and personal transformation is not easy. Finding a tribe to guide me to go deeper was a saving grace. Going deeper is hard to do on our own. It is hard to see beyond our own blind spots and vulnerabilities. I was grateful to find my tribe in *DrivenWoman* during this darker phase of my trajectory.

Curating my own menu of self-care practices became an essential go-to as I relearned to fill my cup. Body scan meditation has been tremendously helpful in bringing my attention to the present moment, experiencing what is taking place in the "here and now," even when I did not like what I was experiencing, such as pain and discomfort.

Living My Purpose

I became an independent HR consultant and assisted organizations that required an injection of human resources management capabilities for clients in the logistics, higher education, projects and engineering, and the government sector. The work has been interesting and fulfilling. I took one small step at a time. I rebuilt the next stage of life. I now draw deep satisfaction from coaching and mentoring others. When faced with life transitions, it is easy to feel paralyzed by not knowing what to do next. There is the fear of failure, fear of change, fear of not having enough, fear of being invisible, fear of losing an identity, and fear of the loss of income, security, and identity. I had been there and knew what it felt like and how to help those paralyzed and stuck move forward.

Doing more than one job gives me satisfaction. It not only uses my skills, and keeps me active and alert, it is financially rewarding too. Embracing a portfolio career is like growing a beautiful garden, with lots of different flowers and plants with different foliage, structures, and textures. I find fulfilment as a life coach to clients from diverse cultures and professional backgrounds. All activities in my varied portfolio are linked in that they are about supporting people and organizations to find more meaning in lifting performance and satisfaction. I find fulfilment in not needing to limit myself to doing the same thing every day. My portfolio "garden" enables individuals and business leaders to build high-performing teams during very challenging times. I have found my own measure of success.

I am drawn to coaching individuals in midlife who are at a turning point in both professional and personal settings. Clients find my lived experience as a spouse of a medical professional relatable, especially when coming out of the pandemic in my mainstream work. **On the surface, clients bring to me challenges like seeking more meaning and purpose, dealing with promotions, or wanting to feel less overwhelmed. The key driver behind this is a deeper, intuitive knowing that there is more to life. I hold the space for my clients and walk beside them on their journey of turning inwards to explore what is truly important.** Paradoxically, doing this work creates the capacity for my clients to acknowledge how resourceful they are. Realizing there is more to life than to-do lists, I work with clients to focus their energies and live a life that feels more meaningful and joyful.

Whilst recovering from trying to be both a *good daughter* and *a good girl,* **I learned the hard way that when working on pleasing others, we lose ourselves.** When we compare ourselves with others, we always find someone who is better than us. Winning in this game of life has little to do with the cards you were dealt; rather, it has more to do with how you play them. **If we focus on ourselves, we can always become better than we were yesterday. As we become better than our past selves, peace of mind and satisfaction return.**

It is my being at peace with my experiences that is turning things around for me. When we stop struggling against something, it changes the whole relationship that gets us through to the other side. In the future, when I order a quilt, you can be assured that I shall be selective to only choose the type of material and color to represent the life I want, and the emotional connections I want with myself and others.

The words of Steve Jobs sum up my experience: "You can't connect the dots looking forward; you can only connect them looking backwards. So, you have to trust that the dots will somehow connect in your future. You have to trust in something—your gut, destiny, life, karma, whatever."

Wisdom Gained from the Journey to Ennoble Business

1. Listening to the whisper within you.
2. Surrounding yourself with your tribe, supporters, and positive influencers.
3. Defining your own measure of success.

Mary Vaz holds the space for her clients and walks beside them on their journey of turning inwards to explore what is truly important. Doing this work creates the curiosity and capacity for her clients to realise and acknowledge how resourceful they are. She works with clients to focus on their priorities and live a life that feels more meaningful and joyful.

As a consummate life coach, HR professional, and medical spouse, Mary is drawn to coaching individuals in midlife who are at a deeper knowing that some things need to change. They may not know yet how things are going to change in both professional and personal settings, but they know they will be an agent of that change. Her clients are from diverse cultures and professional backgrounds.

Mary is a certified member of the Australian Human Resources Institute, holds an Executive MBA from the Australian Graduate School of Management (AGSM), and is now completing a Life Coaching Academy (LCA) Professional Coach ICF NLP program.

Mary lives in Melbourne with her husband, JR, of 27 years. Snowy, their beloved labradoodle is the official well-being advocate in residence.

maryvazlifecoaching@gmail.com
LinkedIn: https://www.linkedin.com/in/mary-vaz-mba-cahri-1b45789/
Instagram: https://www.instagram.com/maryvazlifecoaching/

ROAD TO NOWHERE
BY MANOHARI GUNAWARDHENA

"**Y**ou have great skills, accommodating of other's viewpoints and knowledgeable about your area. You should be in a role which maximizes all three." These were the words of one of my superior officers when I was into 20 plus years of my career. I would have expected and accepted all these words about 5 years into my career, if not less. *What on earth am I doing? Where on earth am I going? Is this the right field or job for me? How can I shine? How can I earn more in the remaining years of my career? How did I end up here?* The questions were whirring around my brain ceaselessly with the danger of slipping into an abyss of self-pity which needed to be avoided at all costs.

I decided to do three things; I am a strong proponent of these three things. It somehow has the ring of finality, a sufficient number to accommodate choices and succinct enough to be coherent.

1. To second guess the so-called positive aspects of my work personality
2. To conduct a critical appraisal of what I think are my positives and negatives as confirmed by people whom I trust (too few of them, alas!)
3. To decide my next course of action to leverage the positives and keep the negatives at bay

Perspective Taking

I am a master at second guessing, deep analysis which borders on conjecture spliced liberally with blinkers. I do have considerable blind spots in analysis. Therefore, I decided "great skills" meant I have nothing specifically good to speak of, "accommodating" meant I was a mouse, and "area expertise" meant I did not know anything else and probably had tunnel vision. The solution to this is to conduct self-analysis.

My skills- I realized one great skill I had was in negotiations in terms of soft skills and time management. I had numeracy and analytics in hard skills. Were they useful to me in my present job role? Yes, of course they were. I was a project leader at most times. I was required to negotiate all the time across, upwards and downwards, both internally and externally. But was I doing it? Not really. The reason was nothing but sheer laziness and fear of rejection. I really needed to overcome the latter. I needed to be rejected. It is good to be rejected. I should have tried to understand why I was rejected so I could have presumably fixed it. I also would have understood what really lied on the other side of failure. I should have spoken with people to build a rapport. This appeared to be hard continuous work. It dawned on me that it would take energy to use my skills with the redeeming factor that since I enjoy talking and persuading people, it would be energy well spent.

External profile- How do I appear mature, inclusive, and approachable yet be taken seriously for my point of view? This was harder than the first. I needed credibility for that. Where was my equity in the organization? I looked carefully at myself. What do people come to me for? A lot of them came for counselling and to bare their hearts. Some asked for my technical advice on how to handle situations and, as expected, some came to me to understand banking and finance issues, which is my area of expertise. Although I felt I was being charitable and accommodating, what was conveyed to me was that I accepted everyone's opinion and made sure my views were nonexistent and got subsumed easily to those of others. I realized that I needed to be strongly committed to my ideas and proposals. It was okay for my ideas to be rejected due to specific reasons, but they should merit serious consideration. In other words, my ideas and proposals may not have been the first or second choice, but at least the third choice. My ideas should not have been off the table so quickly, instead after due consideration, at least synthesized into others' ideas.

Accommodation is a dual-edged sword. My colleagues liked me as I was easier to deal with and their views got accepted, while I have diluted my views and perspectives. My views were associated with me. I had built negative equity in my organization through a series of rejected ideas. Apart from dilution, I was in danger of being taken for granted with a high possibility of happening frequently. Hence, the danger of being ignored was high. Once again, this required hard work, will power, and presentation.

The net result is that I needed to leverage my skills, become more assertive and less easily accommodating, but agree after logical evaluation and a fair negotiation where my ideas are not diluted significantly. I also needed to start looking at how to synthesize ideas instead of choosing one over the other. There was more than a mere duality of choice here. I needed to get off my view of black or white and start embracing the gray scale.

When I entered the banking industry as a trainee straight after university, I had three battles:

1. Female graduate, so cannot be good,
2. Local university and therefore no international exposure, and
3. An ill-mannered boss.

I did not bother about the last two but made sure that I was better than the men. My opportunity came when they had a vacancy in the treasury department of the bank. I aced the selection and got into the holy grail of banking. One manager gave me a long stare and said we used to send our best people to treasury. The message was clear. You are a usurper and soon will stumble and fumble. My first career mistakes were during this period. I could have concentrated on managing people. Instead of managing my boss, I chose to put on a girl guide uniform and fight for what should be, not knowing in my youthful ignorance that what should be is never to be. I've changed my organization four times since then. However, I did not change my career; I stayed in treasury for twenty long years, rising up but not growing much as I did not get lateral useful experience. This meant my natural competencies did not get leveraged. I was getting into a rut and hating it but not understanding how to get out of it.

I had my two kids along the way, which is the biggest joy in my life. I put my career on hold for nearly 6 years, which simply was not necessary as I made some wrong decisions about job changes. I collected some bad and good habits along the way. The good was the networking I did. That has stood the test of time. I made good contacts who taught me, helped me, and motivated me. I became known as a good trainer as I had no fear of public speaking (my passion as yet), which helped me to get to understand people from all levels. Bad habits were the defensiveness and fear of rejection, both of which made me the accommodating mouse which I was perceived to be.

Recommendations to aspirants for success:

1. If someone implies that career is more important than a family, that career is not worth holding on to.
2. Pick your mentor.
3. Learn about the industry and reacted industries of your choice as much as you can by doing anything that comes your way.
4. If the pond is small, do not be scared to join a pool.
5. Trust your instincts.

Embracing the Gray Area

I decided to practice a concept that has always fascinated me, viz Johari window.[19] This theory is based on two ideas—trust can be acquired by revealing information about you to others and learning yourself from their feedback. The first was hard as I never reveal myself easily, although people think I am easy to approach. It is all on the surface. This meant I needed to enhance my vulnerability and get criticized, pigeonholed, but respected in the process. I needed to remove two things in my dealings with others: blind spots and hidden façades. Once I decided, I started moving slowly, painfully and I found it was a relief not to have a hidden façade and was somewhat amazed at the blind spots. The dangers could be avoided. In summary, I decided to embrace the gray that comes with being open, as the kudos of that are trust and empathy.

Striving for Perfection and Accepting Good Enough

Like many of us, I want things to be perfect. I think of having a 22-inch waist and a flat stomach physically and having sufficient energy to get up and go to

---

[19]   https://r.search.yahoo.com/Johari_window/

work after a very long night without any ill effects or weariness. I wish to be on top of everything and understand every little detail, as I am frightened to lose control. I am accepting that physical perfection is a thing of the past, energy levels are just adequate, and most importantly, the means is mostly the end in the journey towards perfection and the end is at times irrelevant.

Journey Forward

I look forward to delivering superior results and justifying the faith some specific people have placed in me no matter what it takes, as I owe it to them. I will be empathetic, irrespective of the fact that it may make my journey slower in superficial terms. I see myself leading with confidence, wisdom, and happiness.

Lesson Learned

I began my career with high goals and expectations and realized competition without relationships is a barren desert of achievement. Empathy and sympathy without credibility will take you on a journey to nowhere but an abyss of self-pity. Honing in on your positives and with perceptions on who you truly are to your stakeholders will help you leverage your skills, enjoy your work, and reach your goals faster. At the end it is worth every effort you make, as you are being you—a better you, a best you, but a true you.

Wisdom Gained from the Journey to Ennoble Business

1. Work hard independent of rewards.
2. Take time to build relationships by opening up to let people in.
3. Be competitive but empathetic and inclusive.

Manohari Gunawardhena is a banker with 30 years' experience in banking, finance, treasury, and capital markets in Sri Lanka and the region.

Her current position is Senior Financial Sector Specialist, South Asia Regional Department, Public Sector Financial Institutions, Asian Development Bank (ADB). She assumed duties in her present capacity in October 2019. Prior to that, she was an Investment Specialist in ADB's Private Sector Operations department covering South Asia, Southeast Asia, Central Asia, and East Asia, specializing in financial institutions for 4 years.

Manohari held corporate management positions as Senior Vice President, Corporate Banking and Capital Markets at DFCC Bank from 2013 to 2015 and the Senior Vice President, Group Treasury and Resource Mobilization of DFCC Bank from 2005 to 2013. In addition to her functional roles, she was also a former non-executive director on the boards of Acuity Securities (Pvt) Limited and Acuity Partners (Pvt) Limited.

Prior to that, she was in leadership roles in National Development Bank, Sri Lanka and Standard Chartered Bank, Colombo branch during her career in treasury/risk and asset and liability management areas in executive management.

Manohari was a former general secretary and vice president of the Sri Lanka Forex Association and a life member of the Association of Professional Bankers, Sri Lanka. She held the position of Secretary General of the APB. She has contributed several articles to the anniversary volume published by the APB. She has been a regular resource person at the Central Bank of Sri Lanka, Training College, and a visiting lecturer at the Colombo University's master's program in Financial Mathematics.

Academically, Manohari is a science graduate from the university of Kelaniya and holds master's degrees in business administration and financial economics from the Postgraduate Institute of Management (PIM) of the Sri Jayewardenepura University and the Colombo University.

eMail: manoharigunawardhena@yahoo.com
LinkedIn: https://www.linkedin.com/in/manohari-gunawardhena-44472539/
Facebook: https://www.facebook.com/manohari.gunawardhena

BUSINESSES THAT COLLABORATE
WILL THRIVE IN THE FUTURE
BY DR. LOIS SONSTEGARD, PHD

D uring the height of the pandemic, when many businesses wondered whether they would survive, I spoke with CEOs, M&A specialists, and a variety of consultants about the pandemic's effects they had seen and what changes they and their clients had made as a result.

My interviews included start-ups and established businesses of all sizes and in a variety of industries. Nearly all of the interviews revealed a common theme: **The key to continued success and future growth for companies of all sizes is collaboration.** Working cooperatively—across silos within your own company, with government entities, non-governmental organizations (NGOs), small community businesses, other organizations in your own and even across industries—would be essential not only to survive the pandemic but to thrive in a post-pandemic world. In fact, the most successful businesses have already begun to see collaboration as the newest asset on their company's balance sheet.

For many companies, collaboration has become as important as IT, their sales channels, and their financing vehicles. It has become an asset because collaboration increases creativity, and creativity increases profitability. Think about what businesses have faced in the past two years with the pandemic creating problems never faced before. CEOs needed to pivot as they determined how to implement and successfully lead a remote workforce, deal with supply chain interruptions, and manage a "new normal" in which the demand for their products and services was unpredictable.

Because of this, creativity has become the number one trait boards of directors, shareholders, and employees look for in CEOs.[20] Recent studies show that collaboration enhances creativity and, ultimately, innovation. In fact, a Department of Industry study found that collaborative industries are 70% more likely to innovate than businesses that don't collaborate. In a study by IBM, 75% of CEOs said that collaboration was important to their innovation efforts. Similarly, 60% of CEOs credited collaboration for leading them to a new way of thinking, which, in turn, led to creative innovation.[21]

More advantages of collaboration

Enhanced creativity and innovation are only the beginning. Collaboration also offers these advantages:

1. **More rapid growth**

It's interesting that we are talking about the need for growth when many businesses are still fighting to survive in a post-pandemic world. But forecasters tell us that, "nearly every marketplace in America is vastly more consolidated than a generation ago," and "economic concentration increasingly blocks entrepreneurs from starting and growing their own businesses."[22] This presents severe challenges, particularly for mid-sized companies that will find it more and more difficult to access the capital and human resources they'll need to grow.

---

[20] deloitte-au-economics-collaborative-economy-google-170614.pdf, p. 14-16, p 29 https://assets.publishing.service.gov.uk/government/uploads/system/uploads/attachment_data/file/272285/6826.pdf and https://www2.deloitte.com/content/dam/Deloitte/au/Documents/Economics/deloitte-au-economics-collaborative-economy-google-170614.pdf p.14-16

[21] IBM. (2008). The new collaboration: enabling innovation, changing the workplace. Accessed 22.04.14 via http://www-935.ibm.com/services/au/cio/pdf/new-collaboration-white-paper.pdf.

[22] The Channel Outlook for 2022: Get Ready for Major Change | Channel Insider. https://www.openmarketsinstitute.org/learn/monopoly-by-the-numbers

When businesses have a collaboration strategy, they are twice as likely to grow faster than their competitors and four times more likely to improve their bottom line.[23] One reason for this rapid growth is an increase in productivity. When Deloitte Access Economics and Deloitte Digital were commissioned by Google to assess collaboration in Australian workplaces, they found that collaborating employees work an average of 15% faster. What's even more significant is that this faster work pace does not sacrifice quality. In fact, Deloitte found that, when employees collaborate 73% of them actually do better work.[24]

Steven Kotler, one of the world's leading experts on human performance, found even more impressive results in his flow research. Kotler defines "getting into the flow" as an optimal state of consciousness where you feel and perform your best. Others describe this state as "being in the zone" or the "runner's high." When you're in the flow, you become so focused on the task at hand that everything else disappears. Kotler's research has shown that when collaborating team members get into the flow, the result is a five-fold increase in productivity. Imagine if your employees could produce in one day what they're currently doing in five days! It's possible when your business facilitates the collaboration of employees across silos within your organization or works collaboratively with other companies in your industry or on a cross-industry basis.

2. **Solutions to complex problems**

Today, businesses face a number of complex problems, many of which are pandemic related. What is required to find the solutions to these problems? I believe there are two things: deep thinking and collaboration among diverse individuals.

In his book *Deep Work: Rules for Focused Success in a Distracted World*, Cal Newport defines "deep work" as the ability to focus without distraction on a cognitively demanding task. This skill enables you to master complicated information quickly and to produce better results in less time. Unfortunately, this skill has become increasingly rare because of all the interruptions we face in today's world of email and social media. Instead of thinking deeply, we're thinking episodically as we are distracted by each email or social media posting.

---

[23]   https://www2.deloitte.com/content/dam/Deloitte/au/Documents/Economics/deloitte-au-economics-collaborative-economy-google-170614.pdf p. 3-5
[24]   https://www2.deloitte.com/content/dam/Deloitte/au/Documents/Economics/deloitte-au-economics-collaborative-economy-google-170614.pdf p. 3-5

It's also important to understand that individuals working on their own tend to make complex problems even more complicated. Collaboration takes a different approach, helping team members do the deep work and truly focus on a complex problem. When you bring together people from diverse companies and backgrounds, they are better able to take apart even the most complex problems. That's essential for the first step to finding a solution: simplify the problem. Collaboration also brings different opinions to the discussion. Only with this kind of input can the problem be put back together again. This time, though, the problem won't look the same as it did before. As a result, it's easier for those tackling the problem to develop a workable solution.

3. **Improved morale**

Employee engagement continues to be a major concern for businesses of all sizes. The most recent numbers show that only 33% of U.S. employees consider themselves fully engaged in their work,[25] and the numbers are actually lower in Europe and Asia. Nearly all businesses have been affected by "The Great Resignation," and we continue to ask if the end is in sight. In study after study, employees tell us that they want to do work that is meaningful and purposeful. They want to know they make a difference and to become a voice that shapes our world for the better.[26] Collaboration provides this opportunity.

The Deloitte study of Australian businesses found that 56% of employees who collaborate are more satisfied with their work. Collaboration has also been found to increase morale by as much as 50%. It's not surprising.[27] When employees collaborate with colleagues in other corporate divisions or at other companies, they get the opportunity to do work that's meaningful, they become more engaged in their work, and they're happier. You get employees who are more productive and more loyal to your company. That's essential as the talent war continues because you'll be able to hire and maintain the right employees to help your business thrive.

---

[25] Changing US Workforce SOAW 2017 FINAL.PDF p. 17
[26] https://www.pewresearch.org/fact-tank/2022/03/09/majority-of-workers-who-quit-a-job-in-2021-cite-low-pay-no-opportunities-for-advancement-feeling-disrespected/
[27] https://www2.deloitte.com/content/dam/Deloitte/au/Documents/Economics/deloitte-au-economics-collaborative-economy-google-170614.pdf p. 3-5

Overcoming the obstacles to collaboration

If collaboration offers so many advantages, why don't more companies collaborate? Part of the answer lies in our culture, particularly in the U.S. and the western world. My own research and studies conducted by others reveals several obstacles:

- **Short-term vs. long-term thinking.** A few years ago, I took a group of business people to Japan and, as introductions were concluding, the Japanese business people asked the Americans about their 200-year plans. The American companies didn't know how to respond because many of them had yet to resolve their five-year plans! To them, a 200-year plan was unthinkable.

  Too much of an emphasis on short-term gains prevents many companies from collaborating. Thought leader and best-selling author Simon Sinek, in his studies of how game theory can apply to business, differentiates between "finite" and "infinite" games.

  A finite game—like football—has fixed rules and a clearly defined end point with winners and losers. In contrast, an infinite game—like business—has changeable rules, and the objective is to keep the game in play. There are no winners or losers, but rather those that drop out of the game—that is, declare bankruptcy—because they've run out of resources or just given up. Because the "game of business" is infinite, we shouldn't act exclusively in our own interests and say things like "we win and you lose." Rather we should act according to our vision and be in it for the long haul. That includes working collaboratively with other companies so that everyone grows.

  Sinek believes great leaders know that it is not about the next quarter or the next election, it's about the next generation and creating an environment in which employees, customers, and shareholders are inspired to keep contributing even after you're gone. Great leaders want to leave their organizations in better shape than they found it. You can only do this by building a business that can survive its leaders.

- **A competitive spirit.** There's nothing wrong with being competitive. But today's challenges call for collaboration. Instead of leading with, "How can I defeat you?" we need to begin thinking, "How can I strengthen you?" That requires us to learn new skills so that we can both grow.

- **Fear and ego.** Another impediment to collaboration is the fear that we will lose our identity and sense of self. Too often, our ego tells us, "I know more than you. My brand is stronger." We can't be afraid to lose our boundaries and turn "I" into "we."

What collaboration has already accomplished

Collaboration isn't a new idea. In the late 19th century, industrialist Andrew Carnegie needed coke, a coal-based fuel, for his steel blast furnaces. Henry Clay Frick owned a successful coke manufacturing company that he wanted to grow. They joined forces: Carnegie got the coke he wanted, and Frick got the money he needed to expand. Frick became chairman of Carnegie Brothers and Company and, in that role, helped build Carnegie into the world's largest manufacturer of steel and coke.

Cal Newport, in his book *Deep Work*, provides another example that illustrates how collaboration can increase speed-to-market. In 1947, Walter Brattain, an experimentalist, and John Bardeen, a quantum theorist, collaborated in a concentrated, focused effort. The result: a series of breakthroughs that led to the first working solid-state transistor.

Perhaps no country has proven the effectiveness of collaboration as much as Japan. After World War II, the Japanese government used collaboration to help companies take the lead in two major industries: automobiles and electronics.[28]

About 15 years ago, I saw Japan again recognize that one way to become an industry leader is by developing collaborative relationships and partnerships. This time their goal was to increase their share of the medical device and pharmaceutical industries. Japanese companies in these industries had grown significantly, but they and the Japanese government were aware that they couldn't go to the next level on their own. A significant commitment of a trillion yen, about $80 billion, was made to develop transpacific partnerships, including developing relationships with similar companies in Minnesota that

---

[28] Phyllis A. Genther. "A History of Japan's Government-Business Relationship: The Passenger Car Industry." Series: *Michigan Papers in Japanese Studies.* Copyright Date: 1990. Published by: University of Michigan Press, U of M Center for Japanese Studies. https://doi.org/10.3998/mpub.18703 Pages: 252 OPEN ACCESS https://www.jstor.org/stable/10.3998/mpub.18703 p. 71

were at the next stage of development—actually bringing products to market. Although this type of long-distance collaboration presents major challenges, the Japanese government and its medical device and pharma companies believe the rewards are worth this major investment.[29] [30]

Perhaps the most widely known recent example of successful collaboration is Operation Warp Speed. This partnership of multiple federal government agencies, pharmaceutical companies, and other organizations resulted in the funding, development, production, and distribution of vaccines for the pandemic much more quickly than it could have been done without the cooperation of all of the entities involved.[31]

Is collaboration part of your strategy?

Every business is unique, and your overall business strategy reflects that. But if you don't have a collaboration strategy in place—or on the drawing board—you're missing an essential asset and resource. Collaboration is essential for basic business survival, and it will soon define a company's future. As Ryunosuke Satoro, a Japanese writer from the early twentieth century, said, "Individually, we are one drop, but together, we are an ocean."

Wisdom Gained from the Journey to Ennoble Business

1. **Success for companies will be determined by their ability to collaborate.**
2. **Collaboration will require new skill sets** – attitudes, values and behaviors that are not familiar in the Western world, which is steeped in competition.
3. **Our world is becoming increasingly complex with more and more complex issues that must be addressed in a collaborative manner.** Individuals and individual organizations no longer have the bandwidth to solve complex problems by themselves.

---

[29] https://www.cao.go.jp/cool_japan/english/pdf/published_document2.pdf
[30] https://spfusa.org/programs/tawaminnesota/
[31] https://www.thelancet.com/journals/langlo/article/PIIS2214-109X(21)00140-6/fulltext

Dr. Lois Sonstegard earned her PhD from the University of Minnesota School of Public Health and has the following as part of her tool kit: Hospital and Health Care Management MBA Carlson School of Management, University of Minnesota, Finance MSN, New York University, Rory Meyers School of Nursing, Parent-Child Health Care Certified as a Coach by organizations such as ICF, Marshall Goldsmith, Gallup, Patrick Lencioni 5 Behaviors of Teams, Leadership Circle, NLP Master Coach, PXT, Personality Tools, Predictive Index, and Scrum.

Through our revolutionary mastermind groups (Collaborative Ecosystems), members step into a group of carefully selected partners committed to the mutual success of each member by addressing together an agreed-upon challenge they want to resolve for their collective benefit. This may be in areas such as supply chain process and access, talent acquisition, and efficient use of resources. By collaborating, members increase their profitability by multiples of what they can do individually.

Imagine the bottlenecks or constraints you face (supply chain, talent acquisition, and access to cash) efficiently managed so you gain time to grow your business and attend to the health of your community and family.

Dr. Sonstegard has experience in Health Care, Manufacturing, Global Distribution, Product Innovation, and Product Launch.

https://build2morrow.com/
https://startwithcollaboration.com
Email: lois.sonstegard@gmail.com
LinkedIn: https://www.linkedin.com/in/loissonstegard/
Twitter: https://twitter.com/lois_sonstegard
YouTube: https://www.youtube.com/c/LoisSonstegardandBuild2Morrow
Facebook: https://www.facebook.com/BuildSuccessCreateLegacy
Instagram: https://www.instagram.com/build2morrow/
Podcast: BuildingMyLegacy

PART THREE

Influence by Design to Thrive

HEALTH AND WELLNESS = BUSINESS SUCCESS
BY DR. SUSILA KULASINGAM

"I *t is 2.30am. I wake up with my thoughts racing, as cortisol and adrenaline, the primary stress hormones, surge through my blood. I reach over for my laptop on my bedside table and by sunrise, I have completed 4 hours of intense work . . . just in time to shower, grab a cup of coffee, and start my normal workday. Next thing I know, it is 10.30pm. I still have tons of work to do, but my body is unable to keep up and my eyelids droop, as I slip into restless slumber, only to awaken again at 2.30am. And the cycle repeats itself. I spend three weekends a month on planes travelling from one international destination to another. I am permanently jet-lagged and my body aches all over, all the time. I fall sick repeatedly with the flu. I can sleep anywhere and everywhere and often do, from sheer exhaustion.*

The work I am doing—finding ways to translate cutting-edge health-related science into real, clinically meaningful improvements and advances in individual and community health—is a passion and my driving force. But . . . while my career is thriving and my spirit is soaring, my health is not. As a physician, I am well aware of the short-term and long-term effects of stress. I realise that I need to recalibrate. I actively seek activities of self-care, nurturing myself and allowing myself periods of peace and quiet. I go for regular full-day bushwalks in state parks, where I immerse myself in the splendour of nature—my spirit rejoicing in the awe of the magnificent

Australian landscape. I resume practicing yoga postures, breathing exercises, and meditation and take-up yoga nidra, a deeply relaxing yoga practise. I actively prioritize time with family and friends. My relationships with people I care about centre me. Our experiences together fill my heart bank and energize me. Collectively, this is the yin *to the* yang *of my life. I work hard and party hard, blazing through this phase of my life with full awareness of what I'm doing. I thrive, living a meaningful, fully engaged life, making sacrifices along the way but through it all, being mindful to take care of myself and my wellbeing. It was an incredibly tough and challenging period, but it was also one of the most astonishingly awesome periods of my life, one which would not have been possible without good health and wellbeing."*

So what? In the global business world, many successful leaders are increasingly acknowledging and espousing the value of health, wellbeing, and self-care.[32][33][34] The World Health Organization defines health as "a state of complete physical, mental, and social well-being and not merely the absence of disease or infirmity."[35] It goes on to refer to four factors—personal (factors such as genetics, diet, physical activity, smoking, alcohol consumption, and drug use), social (factors such as relationships, networks, and community), economic (factors such as education, employment, income, power) and environmental (factors such as air, water, housing, neighbourhood, transport, parks, and nature reserves)—which influence health status.[36] Clearly, health is multi-dimensional. It is complicated, with some factors within our control and others not. We live in an incredible period of unprecedented advances in medicine and surgery. Our life expectancy has increased dramatically over the centuries. But now, the leading causes of death globally are consequent to tobacco use, high blood pressure, high blood sugar, physical inactivity, overweight/obesity, and excessive alcohol consumption.[37] All largely lifestyle diseases, leading to premature illness and death. Thankfully, we can turn this tide with some simple things we can do ourselves to enable good health and well-being.

---

[32] *7 Business Leaders Share Their Self-Care Secrets.* https://www.forbes.com/sites/rhettpower/2020/09/20/7-business-leaders-share-their-self-care-secrets/?sh=369b58c5309d
[33] *The health-savvy CEO.* Deloittte Insights. https://www2.deloitte.com/us/en/insights/topics/leadership/ceo-role-employee-health-wellness.html
[34] *Employers See wellness Link to Productivity, Performance.* SHRM. https://www.shrm.org/resourcesandtools/hr-topics/benefits/pages/wellness-productivity-link-.aspx
[35] World Health Organization Constitution, 1948. https://www.who.int/about/governance/constitution\
[36] Ibid.
[37] The top 10 causes of death. World Health Organisation. https://www.who.int/news-room/fact-sheets/detail/the-top-10-causes-of-death

How? Japan, Spain, and Italy are amongst the healthiest countries in the world.[38] In Japan, their traditional diet is low in red meat and high in fish and vegetables and they maintain a way of life that encourages people to have strong social networks and stay connected with nature.[39][40] The famed Mediterranean diet, based primarily on vegetables, fruits and nuts with small amounts of fish, is believed to be a key reason for the high health rankings of Spain and Italy.[41][42] Blue zones are geographic areas in the world where the healthiest populations live. Here are some of the defining characteristics common to the people who live in these areas:[43]

- they eat wisely and moderately, mostly a plant-based diet
- physical activity is incorporated into their lifestyles consequential to their environment
- they live purposeful lives
- their relationship with themselves, their loved ones, and their community is strong
- they incorporate moments of solitude, joy, peace, or prayer, which help them manage the stress in their lives
- any alcohol consumption is moderate

"*Kanyini*" refers to the principle of wholeness and connectedness through responsibility and care.[44] It is dependent on four aspects: "*tjukurrpa*" (the right way to live), "*ngura*" (a sense of belonging to the land), "*walytja*" (family), and "*kurunpa*" (spirituality). An intrinsic abiding philosophy of the First Nations peoples of Australia, it speaks to the interconnectedness of life. Everything is one. You cannot be well if your community is unwell or if the earth and nature are sick. Health and well-being are inextricably linked to that which is around us.

Personally, I draw inspiration from my own heritage of *Sanatana Dharma*,[45] a venerated ancient way of life passed down through the generations. It incorporates the practise of yoga, comprising the philosophy, principles and practises of

[38] *These are the world's healthiest nations.* World Economic Forum. https://www.weforum.org/agenda/2019/02/these-are-the-world-s-healthiest-nations/
[39] Ibid.
[40] *Okinawa's Longevity Lessons.* https://www.bluezones.com/press/okinawas-longevity-lessons/
[41] *These are the world's healthiest nations.* World Economic Forum. https://www.weforum.org/agenda/2019/02/these-are-the-world-s-healthiest-nations/
[42] *Why the Mediterranean Diet for heart health?* https://www.heartresearch.com.au/mediterranean-diet
[43] *Reverse Engineering Longevity.* https://www.bluezones.com/2016/11/power-9/
[44] *Kanyini.* http://www.kanyini.com/
[45] Flood G. *An Introduction to Hinduism.* Cambridge University Press 1996.

yama (moral standards such as truthfulness and non-violence), *niyama* (observances such as cleanliness, contentment, self-awareness), *asana* (physical postures), *pranayama* (breath control), *pratyahara* (sensory withdrawal), *dharana* (mindfulness), *dhyana* (meditation), and *samadhi* (peace).[46] Collectively, they form the bedrock of holistic health and well-being for me and, importantly, my place in society and the world. Nowadays, the term yoga is used to refer to *asana*, the physical postures of yoga, which by itself offers various proven benefits including reducing stress, increasing flexibility and balance, improving heart health, and aiding with rest and sleep.[47]

By now, it should be clear that health is not just about eating the "right" food and exercising. Whilst important, holistic health necessitates the incorporation of favourable physical, mental, spiritual, and emotional aspects into our lifestyles. Strong, healthy relationships have been found to reduce mental and physical health issues. Conversely, loneliness and social isolation increase the risk of premature death, dementia, depression, heart disease, and stroke, amongst others.[48] A recent Harvard Business Review article highlighted the importance of preserving our sense of wonderment, with a call to action of taking "awe walks," listing benefits such as stress reduction, increasing creativity and innovation, and better resilience, amongst others.[49] Creative pursuits such as music, dance, and the arts have been shown to enhance wellbeing. Amongst others, they were shown to reduce anxiety, pain, and blood pressure.[50] Mindfulness, being in the moment without judgment, has also been shown to help reduce stress, anxiety and negativity.[51] So, there are a plethora of "healthy" choices you can incorporate into your life.

When? For me, a holistic, healthy lifestyle was part of the fabric of my upbringing. For most of us, though, we start to think about health when our body breaks down

---

[46] Bryant E.F. *The Yoga Sutras of Patanjali.* North Point Press 2009.
[47] *9 Benefits of Yoga.* Johns Hopkins Medicine. https://www.hopkinsmedicine.org/health/wellness-and-prevention/9-benefits-of-yoga
[48] *Social Isolation and Loneliness.* World Health Organisation. https://www.who.int/teams/social-determinants-of-health/demographic-change-and-healthy-ageing/social-isolation-and-loneliness
[49] *Why You Need to Protect Your Sense of Wonder – Especially Now.* Harvard Business Review. https://hbr.org/2021/08/why-you-need-to-protect-your-sense-of-wonder-especially-now
[50] *Can you dance your way to better health and well-being? For the first time, WHO studies the link between the arts and health.* World Health Organisation. https://www.euro.who.int/en/media-centre/sections/press-releases/2019/can-you-dance-your-way-to-better-health-and-well-being-for-the-first-time,-who-studies-the-link-between-arts-and-health
[51] *What are the benefits of mindfulness?* American Psychological Association. https://www.apa.org/monitor/2012/07-08/ce-corner

and we fall ill. If you take the example of bone health, we only worry about it when we get older and the risk of falls increase, potentially resulting in fractures. Our bodies, however, have their own growth trajectory. Our bone density peaks at around the age of 30 and is stable for the next 20 years or so, then begins to decrease.[52] So, in fact, it is in your best interest to build strong bones early in life by ensuring good nutrition and regular exercise in your early years. But how many of us think about our bone health in our 20s or 30s? I don't know about you, but I had all sorts of other things on my mind at that age. Thankfully, my upbringing afforded me aspects of nutrition and movement which were and are part of my routine life. If you didn't get the benefit of this, it's never too late to start right now—for yourself and your children. Make the effort now and habitualize good practises, so it becomes a part of your lifestyle. It will then require very little on-going thought and set you and, critically, your future generations up for success—just as my parents did for me.

Where do I start? *Deciding how to nurture ourselves starts with an awareness and understanding of what matters to you. Being well encompasses living in alignment with what you value.* I use a simple way to think about this, drawing parallels with a rechargeable battery . . . energy in, energy out. For a rechargeable battery to function, it needs to be charged. As it is utilised, the energy gets depleted, so it needs to be charged again. But what is the source of this "energy" for us? Is it physical exercise? Is it money? Is it a delicious, nutritious meal? Is it the vision of a beautiful sunrise? Is it meaningful work? Is it having a good belly laugh with your mates? Is it frolicking in the surf? Is it cuddling your babies/fur-babies first thing in the morning? Is it the wind in your hair as you ride your bicycle along a parkland? Is it brilliant blue skies and fresh air? I know what it is for me. Do you? Do you know what makes you feel strong and confident, your heart bank overflowing with awe, wonder, joy, serenity, passion, vigor . . . all those things that inspire, nourish, and invigorate you? This is your energy source—cultivate it.

Why? The American poet, Mary Oliver, asked, "Tell me, what is it you plan to do with your one wild and precious life?" I started this chapter with a story about a period in my life when I was clearly a workaholic, burning the candle at both ends and pushing my boundaries. The choices I made, however, were intentional and deliberate, knowing it would be for a finite period. Accordingly, I made space in my life for self-care, centering, and nurturing. I checked in with myself regularly and recalibrated as I needed to. **My invitation to you is that once you decide what you plan to do with your "one wild and precious**

---

[52] *Bone health: Tips to keep your bones healthy.* Mayo Clinic. https://www.mayoclinic.org/healthy-lifestyle/adult-health/in-depth/bone-health/art-20045060

life," you also intentionally nurture yourself to be in a good space to achieve it.

No one is better placed than you to ensure this. **As the saying goes, you hold the pen that writes the story of your life. So, choose deliberately, align with what gives meaning to your life, be healthy and well, and go forth and write your beautiful story.**

Wisdom Gained from the Journey to Ennoble Business

1. Good health and wellbeing are foundational to your success in life and in business.
2. You are responsible for your health.
3. Incorporate things which nurture your physical, spiritual, mental, and emotional health into your lifestyle, so they become your norm.

Dr. Susila Kulasingam is a healthcare professional whose passion for health and well-being stems from her own personal journey through life and from the intimately intertwined journeys of her family and friends. She draws inspiration from her experiences with her patients—as a clinician early in her career, from her experiences with her fellow corporate colleagues—as a Pharmaceutical Physician Executive within Research and Development-based Fortune 500 pharmaceutical companies for over 15 years, and from her experiences with her community—as a public health advocate and educator. Susila has a medical degree (MBBS, India), as well as master's degrees in Pharmaceutical Medicine (MScPharmMed, Ireland) and Public Health (MPH, Australia).

Based in Sydney, Australia, Susila is an avid walker and swimmer, reads voraciously, loses herself in her piano-playing, practices and teaches yoga, finds awe in discovering new things about the people and world around her and laughs often at the antics of her little dog, Layla.

LinkedIn: www.linkedin.com/in/susila-kulasingam-335a283

TRANSCENDENT CULTURE: THE KEY TO RECRUITING AND RETAINING WOMEN LEADERS
BY KAREN ANN BULLUCK

A recent McKinsey & Co. survey "found that in the early days of the [pandemic], one in four women were considering leaving their jobs. Today, that average is up to one in three. For women with children, it could be even worse."[53] Over 2.3 million women have left the workforce in the last two years, a trend that started before the pandemic but worsened rapidly during it. And all this is happening at a time when corporations are being pressured to increase the gender diversity of their senior leadership teams and boards.

Why are so many women opting out of corporate life? The same McKinsey survey found that women leaders appear to be more burnt out than men. "Despite this added stress and exhaustion, women are rising to the moment as stronger leaders and taking on the extra work that comes with this: compared with men at the same level, women are doing more to support their teams and advance diversity, equity, and inclusion efforts. They are also more likely to be

[53] Morris, C. *World Reimagined: The Pandemic Drives Women and Mothers Out of the Workforce.* NASDAQ Online. https://www.nasdaq.com/articles/world-reimagined%3A-the-pandemic-drives-women-and-mothers-out-of-the-workforce-2021-10-04

allies to women of color. Yet this critical work is going unrecognized and unrewarded by most companies, and that has concerning implications. Companies risk losing the very leaders they need right now."[54]

In my work, I've spoken with dozens of women who have left corporate to start their own businesses, retire, or focus on their families. Most of them don't plan to go back. They just can't tolerate the toxic cultures and the lack of recognition and support for the work they are doing any longer. The chronic stress, the fatigue, and the constant battle to meet unrealistic goals have worn thin, and women are saying, "Enough." The money, the perks, are not enough. They're choosing to take care of themselves and their families in different ways. It honestly saddens and frightens me to hear their stories. Corporations need these leaders. It's not just a loss for organizations. It's a loss for all of us.

A solution is available. But it's not an easy one, because the solution requires changing the way corporate leaders approach business, management, and yes, even life. Throwing money at the problem through traditional leadership development programs, aggressive recruiting, and exorbitant salaries isn't working, but few leaders know what will.

I believe and have found that what will work is a fundamental change in corporate cultures. A change that we might not have felt comfortable discussing a few years ago. But the pandemic and the ensuing shift in people's attitudes and expectations are changing the conversation.

What is needed now to recruit and retain the female leaders that corporations desperately need is the creation of a Transcendent Culture. A transcendent culture values people, fosters innovation, and makes positive changes in the lives of their employees, their communities, and society at large. There's been much debate about the role of corporations, who their stakeholders really are. Traditionalists maintain that the corporate goal is solely making money for the shareholders. But in today's multi-national, multi-cultural world, making money is more complex than it's ever been. Competitive advantage is harder to attain and maintain, and people are looking beyond the bottom line to assess what impact on the world companies are having, and that includes employees and consumers alike.

---

[54] Burns, T, Huang, J. et al. *Women in the Workplace 2021*. McKinsey & Co. https://www.mckinsey.com/featured-insights/diversity-and-inclusion/women-in-the-workplace

A Transcendent Culture sees beyond the narrow confines of the bottom line, not ignoring it, but understanding that the reality of success is much more nuanced and expansive than the numbers in an annual report or the current stock price. Those are short-term and, often, short-sighted measures of success. Company leaders who are in it for the long haul are looking beyond those measures and seeing where the value really is: in people, in connection, and in strengthening the whole.

Transcendent Culture Starts With Transcendent Leaders

Any discussion of a Transcendent culture must begin with understanding what a Transcendent leader is. Culture always starts at the top of an organization, and this is especially true with cultural change. As noted by Grant Freeland, "Culture change comes from concrete and noticeable changes in leadership behavior."[55] Therefore, leaders must change first because it's the leaders that influence the tone, the mindset, and the beliefs of the corporation.

Many companies start with an inspirational mission statement and a set of corporate values meant to set the tone and guide the behavior of the employees. And there's nothing wrong with those things. They are very valuable tools for communicating culture to new employees, suppliers, and customers. But as the old saying goes, actions speak louder than words. For the mission and values statement to have any meaning, the leaders must *embody* them.

How does that happen? A Transcendent leader starts with the awareness of a higher level of consciousness, that unseen yet all-important realm beyond the bounds of normal human consciousness. The final version of Maslow's hierarchy of needs, which is rarely shown, included a sixth level: Transcendence. He recognized that this final level of human evolution refers to "the highest and most inclusive or holistic levels of human consciousness."[56] At this level of consciousness, we become aware that we are not separate entities but are connected to each other, to all living things, and to the cosmos in which we live. Science, in the form of quantum mechanics, has proven this as fact. Yet, it's a

[55] Freeland, G. *Cultural Change: It Starts at the Top.* Forbes Online. July 2016. https://www.forbes.com/sites/grantfreeland/2018/07/16/culture-change-it-starts-at-the-top/?sh=68f16fac36c
[56] Maslow, A.F. The Farther Reaches of Human Nature, New York, 1971.

level of consciousness in which few understand and fewer still operate. But the connection to and faith in this higher level of consciousness is a foundational aspect of being a Transcendent leader.

This connection has been described and documented for centuries in the world's wisdom traditions, great and small. It has been called "universal consciousness," "Source," or the myriad of names that people have chosen for a divine entity. It doesn't matter how you name it. The value is in the faith, the trust, the belief in something larger than yourself, in the larger whole in which we are all enmeshed. To be a Transcendent leader, you must be able to tap into this level of consciousness and the wisdom, creativity, and connection to others that it invokes.

We can turn to the world's wisdom traditions and the current understanding of mindfulness for ways to make and nurture that connection. Meditation, centering prayer, journaling, and walks in nature are all methods that both ground us in our connection and elevate our way of being. They create touchstones for us to return to time after time to spark new ideas, receive answers to complex problems, and approach ourselves and others with love and compassion.

Transcendent leaders also have a deep awareness of their beliefs, cultural conditioning, and biases. These are the beliefs that create blind spots. With this awareness, leaders are able to identify and shift out of these minefields in their minds when they are negatively impacting their ability to listen, empathize, and make decisions. This is the inner work of leadership. So often, it is our own unconsciously held beliefs that get in our way, that stop us from being effective, from nurturing those around us, and from hearing the key information that helps us navigate uncertainties in the world. Awareness allows us to challenge those beliefs that limit us and uproot the ideas lodged in our consciousness that slow us down. Transcendent leaders uplift and empower others, and this deep awareness of their beliefs is an important prerequisite to do so.

Clarity is the third pillar of my Transcendent leadership methodology. In many ways, clarity stems from the connection to universal consciousness and from awareness of one's own limiting beliefs, but it has a place of its own. People in organizations expect vision, direction, and a perspective they can embrace and enhance. But clarity is more than just Vision. Transcendent leaders must have clarity about who they are as a person, what their values are, and what's important to them and their future. Rock-solid in their understanding of themselves, leaders with clarity not only inspire but are also able to listen, incorporate the ideas of others, and allow their vision to expand and grow because they don't need to defend themselves. They know who they are and what they stand for, and they embody it fully. They shift from "doing leadership" to "being a leader."

How does being a Transcendent leader help keep women engaged?

You read a lot about feminine leadership skills, how they're needed, how they're missing. I'm sure there are some who would label Transcendent leadership as being "feminine leadership." It's not. Women are not the only ones who can be compassionate, empathetic, and connected to higher consciousness. However, women are historically socialized to be compassionate and empathetic. Many female leaders in corporations have felt enormous pressure <u>not</u> to be so compassionate and empathetic. I know I did. The rational, detached style of leadership that we've seen up until now has largely worked. When something appears to be working, people don't change it. They try to emulate it.

However, the flaws with the rational, traditional model of leadership became more apparent during the pandemic. Leaders faced emotional and spiritual challenges in unprecedented ways, both for themselves and their employees. I found this quote from a participant in the McKinsey study informative:

"It's the only time of my career that I seriously considered a less demanding job. I took another interview. I felt burned out so often. I felt caught in the middle of everyone's emotional response to the pandemic and in between decision-makers who have very, very different outlooks on how to respond. It was the first time I had to solve problems that so directly impacted people's mental and physical health. It was the hardest working year of my life."
—Female senior vice president[57]

Many, many leaders were ill-equipped to deal with the levels of stress and trauma that the pandemic caused. The reference to "decision-makers who had very, very different outlooks on how to respond" is very telling. When corporate leaders are all going different directions, that kind of chaos is the

---

[57] Burns, T, Huang, J. et al. *Women in the Workplace 2021.* McKinsey & Co. https://www.mckinsey.com/featured-insights/diversity-and-inclusion/women-in-the-workplace

result, and it increases the stress on everyone. With connection, awareness, and clarity, Transcendent leaders can literally transcend (rise above) this kind of emotional chaos and draw answers from universal wisdom and not their own limited experiences.

A Transcendent culture is truly inclusive, accepting everyone's strengths and weaknesses, and supportive and flexible enough to allow employees to thrive. This culture will attract and retain the men and women who are ready to operate on the next level, with ease and grace accomplishing more than the pushing and prodding of the 'carrot and stick' mentality that has dominated leadership for centuries. Once we understand the true, inner connectedness of life and each other, we have the power to harness that energy in ways that we never could have imagined.

The Path Forward

The emotional stakes of trying to lead in a culture that's not conducive to one's values, perspective and modality are daunting. Many women have tried and failed. Unable to change the culture, they leave or take a different kind of role. The pandemic only accelerated this trend. **The time is now to change, to pivot and embrace a new way of leadership, where "being a leader" is more important than "doing leadership."**

To get you started, here are three important things I've learned about the journey to a Transcendent Culture:

1. Culture starts at the top of the organization. The highest-level leaders must engage in changing themselves first.
2. Connection to universal consciousness is the key to achieving real transcendence, real change. It's also the key to realizing your full potential and achieving the best results.
3. Leadership is more about who you are being than what you are doing. If you are connected, aware, and clear about who you are, your words and actions will follow. For a Transcendent leader, "being" always precedes "doing."

Karen Ann Bulluck is a transcendent leadership specialist and founder of *TRANSCENDENCE: Living A Life of Meaning*, a boutique executive coaching practice. Karen partners with leaders to EXPLORE what matters, INTEGRATE the higher self, and FLOURISH in new dimensions. She is the creator of the Transcendence proprietary methodology: "Living A Life of Meaning," which provides transformative and integrative teachings learned from three decades of applied practice.

Karen was the first woman promoted to Executive Vice President at AM Best Company, the premier international insurance rating agency and information provider. Karen was a member of the board of directors for the AM Best Europe Information Services subsidiary and the parent company. Her career was marked by rapid promotions and many cross-disciplinary changes.

She specialized in bringing innovation and change to struggling departments: upgrading technology, redefining processes, and aligning the right staff with the right jobs.

Karen earned a Master of Science in Organization Leadership with honors from Regis University, Denver CO, her professional coaching certification from iPEC, and her undergraduate degree from at the University of Virginia. She has immersed herself in the study of the world's wisdom traditions and leadership models.

She is the author of the Amazon bestselling novel *Ascending Ladders*, which follows a female executive through a transformation change in corporate leadership. Karen is also a contributing author to the international bestselling books: *Significant Women: Leaders Reveal What Matters Most* and *The X-Factor: The Spiritual Secrets Behind Successful Executives & Entrepreneurs*.

Email: karen@livingalifeofmeaning.com
Website: https://livingalifeofmeaning.com
LinkedIn: https://www.linkedin.com/in/karenannbulluck/
Facebook: https://www.facebook.com/karenannbulluck
Twitter: https://twitter.com/KarenAnnBulluck

ELEVATING THE HUMAN SIDE OF ENTERPRISE
BY ROBIN LITSTER JOHNSON

I n a powerful scene from the movie *A Christmas Carol*, starring George C. Scott[58], a stunned and frightened Ebenezer Scrooge attempts to console the despairing apparition of his long-dead business partner, Jacob Marley, by meekly saying, "You always were a good man of business." To which Marley roars in response, "*Business?? Mankind was my business!* The common welfare was my business. Charity, mercy, forbearance, and benevolence were *all my business!*"

Does "the common welfare"—considering the well-being of those around us, valuing the group as a whole—merit a valid place on the agendas of successful CEOs, CFOs, and profitable companies? Is the notion of having "charity, mercy, forbearance, and benevolence" in professional organizations merely the raving of an imaginary ghost in a work of fiction, or do those principles have science-backed and evidence-based foundations which "men of business" ignore today at their peril? Is there truly a measurable ROI on organizational resilience and on positive, ennobled leadership emanating from the C-suite?

---

[58] Fuisz, R. E., Kelman, A. R. & Storke, G. F. (Producers), Donner, C. (Director). (1984). *A Christmas Carol* [Motion Picture]. United States: Entertainment Partners Ltd.

A quick perusal of today's academic studies and financial literature delivers a resounding "Yes!" _Every_ business strategy is ultimately created and implemented by human beings, and an abundance of research[59] [60] [61] shows that leaders and organizations that are "Humane, Ethical, and Resilient"[62]—taking into account "the common welfare" and manifesting "charity, mercy, forbearance, and benevolence"—are far more likely to succeed in the marketplace. Industrial Age, top-down, dictatorial styles of leadership are less effective—and likely ineffective—in today's work environment.

From the dramatic to the banal, myriad success stories in business, government, and non-profits alike demonstrate that elevating the human side of enterprise often spells the difference between long-term success and underachievement, or even disaster. In the following examples from around the globe, we can discover common, science-backed principles that can be learned by leaders at every level, and evidence-based practices that can be applied within organizations both large and small, regardless of geographic location.

Rocky Flats

The transformation of the Rocky Flats Nuclear Weapons Production Facility in Colorado, United States into the Rocky Flats National Wildlife Refuge is one of the most dramatic turnarounds in organizational history.[63] [64] The facility was catapulted from utter disaster on every level to extraordinary success that went well beyond the predictions of even the most ardent optimists.

Having been established in 1952 during the Cold War, much of the Rocky Flats workforce included multiple generations of employees. They held fierce pride in their sense of mission and the level of skill required to make nuclear

[59] Cameron, K. (2012). Positive leadership: Strategies for extraordinary performance ed. 2. Berrett-Koehler.
[60] Dutton, J. E., & Spreitzer, G. M. (Eds.). (2014). How To Be A Positive Leader - Insights from Leading Thinkers on Positive Organizations. Berrett-Koehler Publisher.
[61] Greenberg, M. H. & Maymin, S. (2013). Profit from the positive: Proven leadership strategies to boost productivity and Transform Your Business. McGraw-Hill Education.
[62] Johnson, R. (2017). _Robin Learning Systems._ https://robinlearningsystems.com.
[63] Cameron, K. S. & Lavine, M. (2006). Making the impossible possible: Leading extraordinary performance–the rocky flats story. Berrett-Koehler Publishers.
[64] Cameron, K. (2012). Positive leadership: Strategies for extraordinary performance ed. 2. Berrett-Koehler.

weapons, which included working with the most dangerous substances on the planet. Despite this, the facility was riven with discord and distrust between the workers, represented by three different labor unions, and management. There were hundreds of grievances and complaints filed each year, and multiple safety violations were recorded.

The animosity did not stop at the razor wire fence surrounding the 800 buildings ironically situated on 6000 acres within a verdant valley in Colorado. The local community was openly antagonistic toward the facility and had been so for decades. Armed guards kept vocal protestors at bay, but not out of sight nor earshot. Hostilities were also regularly exchanged with government regulators and other Department of Energy sites throughout the country. In a word, acrimony, suspicion, and combativeness permeated almost every connection point inside and outside the facility.

In 1989 the FBI raided and shut down the facility due to suspicions of undocumented pollution. The workers, who still had to report to work but had nothing to do, felt immediately stripped of their sense of mission and purpose. When the nuclear weapons program at Rocky Flats was permanently discontinued in 1992, morale was at an all-time low. It was determined by government regulators that it would take 70 years and $36 billion to "clean up the mess" at Rocky Flats.

However, Kaiser-Hill (parent company CH2MHill), the contracting company chosen to close Rocky Flats, applied principles and practices of sound organizational scholarship and ennobled, positive leadership, and instead of 70 years and $36 billion, the cleanup process at Rocky Flats took *only six years and only $6 billion*, and the Refuge became 13 times cleaner than was required by law.

The plant workers, labor union representatives, management executives, community leaders, environmental activists, and government regulators were enabled to come together and were motivated to collaborate and cooperate in this massive redemptive process. Eventually they together envisioned and then created the Rocky Flats National Wildlife Refuge—a place of life and abundance where once existed a nuclear weapons facility focused on death and destruction.

Extraordinary, bottom-line results, indeed . . . and we shall see that these results are not isolated to Rocky Flats, but have manifested themselves in multiple ways that have made a global impact.

Saudi Telecom

On the other side of the world, both geographically and politically, the transformation of Saudi Telecom (STC) from a government-owned ministry to a for-profit private company was nothing short of astonishing (Cameron, 2021). The Saudi Kingdom realized it needed to move from relying primarily on oil and gas resources for revenue to be a more digital based economy. The telecommunications ministry, completely controlled by the Saudi monarchy, was selected for the Kingdom's first foray into privatization. Khaled H. Biyari was appointed CEO in 2015, and was hugely instrumental in the organization's turnaround.

In 2013, the McKinsey Consulting firm had given STC one of the lowest "organizational health" scores in the world—a 33 out of 100. By 2018, it had skyrocketed to a score of 71, the largest five-year increase in McKinsey history. Also in 2018, the Arabian Society for Human Resource Management named STC the "Best Talent Program in the Gulf" for its High Potential Development Program created for its employees. These human resource milestones were reflected in dollars and cents: its stock market value doubled between 2015 and 2020, while their competitors' shares dropped 50%, and its brand value grew from $2.8 billion to $6.2 billion. In 2021, it was one of the top three brands in the Middle East, serving at least 11 countries.

A Small Non-Profit in Los Angeles

A small non-profit music education coalition in Los Angeles, United States, was founded by a music teacher genuinely passionate about helping children learn music. Through sheer grit and force of will, she built the organization to include several teachers, dozens of children, and multiple instruments. This "force of will" proved to be a two-edged sword, however, and eventually, teacher after teacher left the group, taking their private students with them, and the organization dwindled by two-thirds. Finally, most of the last few teachers also threatened to leave if significant changes were not made at the top.

With the organization then in its 40th year, its demise would have been tragic: hundreds of children over the years, including now-professional musicians, had their roots in this musical enterprise. Fortunately, a few of the remaining teachers stepped up and began applying principles of sound leadership and organizational scholarship. The original founder was encouraged to step aside and assume the role of Director Emeritus. With new, positive leadership, all the remaining teachers deeply and extensively discussed the vision and purpose of their organization. They surveyed the parents and children to find out what they liked best about the activities and focus, and how the organization could be improved to fulfill its vision and expand its reach. With this new enthusiasm and positive direction, the organization began to revive and became a place where students, parents, and teachers love to participate.

During the global pandemic that began in March 2020, many similar music education coalitions in the area simply stopped providing services because of lockdowns in the United States. However, the leaders and teachers of this coalition were fiercely determined to continue bringing the joy of music to their students, and to be a bright spot for these children whose lives had been so drastically upended. For well over a year, they taught music lessons online, creatively adapting their methods, and providing additional Parent Support Forums on topics such as resilience and motivation. After the pandemic restrictions were eased and live lessons resumed, they used positive principles and practices to reintegrate the group. They are now planning the 50th anniversary of the organization, to take place in 2024. **Again, principles of ennobled leadership and positive practices revived an organization that had once looked doomed.**

Science-backed Principles

How did these three organizations achieve such astonishing results, even though the organizations were from very different business, geographic, and cultural contexts? They did so by using ennobled leadership principles which transcend time, location, and culture, and by applying positive practices which embody those principles. What are some of the universal truths and science-backed principles common to these diverse turn-around situations? They include:

- humility within leaders at all levels
- positively energizing relationships and relationship networks
- strengths-based approach to problem solving
- values-based decision making
- flexibility/adaptability

- institutionalized forgiveness
- gratitude and generosity

In a word, looking toward "the common welfare" and having "charity, mercy, forbearance, and benevolence" for everyone within the organization.

Wisdom Gained from the Journey to Ennoble Business

What are some of the golden nuggets of wisdom gleaned from the journeys described above which can be applied by organizations in diverse locations, cultures, and political realities? While there are a plethora of concrete, evidence-based practices (Cameron, 2012, 2021; Dutton, 2003; Dutton & Spreitzer, 2014; Greenberg & Greenlee, 2021; Greenberg & Maymin, 2013), here are three which I have personally used and found to be most potent:

1. Be fiercely committed to the positive and the unseen possible.

In the small non-profit music coalition described above, I was the only teacher who believed the founder would completely step aside, while the rest were ready to walk away and try to start a new group. I said, "We *must* try. We must *try*." The request for significant organizational change was made and eventually accepted, and I was able to help lead the group in a new direction, infusing it with positive principles and revitalizing practices.

At Rocky Flats, during the very first meeting convened by Kaiser-Hill/CH2MHill with Rocky Flats personnel, despite the background of rancor, distrust, and animosity, a Senior Executive said to the entire group, "This is the best team I've ever worked with . . ."[65] He saw the unseen possible, focused on the positive, and helped lead the way to extraordinary results.

2. Use the three D's of listening: Listen Diversely, Deeply, and Determinedly.

Talk with and listen to a *diverse* set of stakeholders—those who help make the decisions, those who have to implement the decisions, and those who will be affected by the decisions—both inside and outside of the organization itself.

---

[65] Cameron, K. S. & Lavine, M. (2006). Making the impossible possible: Leading extraordinary performance–the rocky flats story. Berrett-Koehler Publishers. 181.

Listen *deeply* and seriously to what this diverse group has to say, why they feel the way they do, why they hold their various perspectives, and get their ideas for improving the organization. Listen with upfront and overt *determination* to implement as many of these ideas as possible, even if some of them need to be implemented over the long term.

3. Create a Culture of Generosity.

From the C-Suite to the janitors, model and encourage behavior where people willingly share time, energy, knowledge, skills, ideas, and connections with each other. Eliminate or reduce scarcity-minded "silo-ism" where people hoard information and resources. Openly "give credit where credit is due" and acknowledge contributions made by those who genuinely help but are often overlooked.

Conclusion

In looking at the transformation of the organizations described above, the words of Jason Lauritsen (Lauritsen, 2010), who compared the modern world of work with being stuck in The Matrix, are deeply inspiring:

". . . the traditional way we've inherited to manage and organize work is like The Matrix. We've been stuck inside this inhuman, and frequently inhumane, model of work for so long that most don't realize that there is an alternative. . . It is time to do away with the inhumane and ineffective management practices of the past, and to accept a new reality. . ."

I am passionate about teaching and inspiring organizations to be more Humane, Ethical, and Resilient, and am completely committed to the belief that businesses and organizations can be ennobling forces for good. Together we can elevate the human side of enterprise.

As a Resilience and Wellbeing Advisor, I am passionate about teaching and inspiring organizations to become more Humane, Ethical, and Resilient. I have taught organizational resilience and leadership skills to numerous professional organizations, and believe that business can be—and should be—a force for good in the world. I am a leader of various non-profit organizations, and have used the science of wellbeing to help them become more Humane, Ethical, and Resilient.

I teach individuals to build inner resilience, and to discover and develop personal character strengths, creating a life of thriving, not just surviving. I have taught principles and practices of wellbeing to patrons of the YWCA, various church groups, and individuals, and have seen the power of those concepts and skills to transform lives for the better.

As a fraud prevention expert, I work with SAFEChecks and am the primary Editor of Frank Abagnale's *Fraud Bulletin*, which is used by the FBI, Federal Reserve, and organizations throughout the country. I believe all fraud is ultimately human in nature, and that fraud prevention protocols and practices are most effective when they appropriately address the human side of enterprise.

To round things out, I am a Suzuki violin teacher and a Co-Director of the Suzuki Music Program of Los Angeles. To quote Pablo Casals, "Perhaps it is music that will save the world. . ." Along with the science of wellbeing!

I have three amazing daughters and sons-in-law, and two delightful granddaughters, and am profoundly grateful for their love and support.

Email Address: Robin@RobinLearningSystems.com
Phone Number: (818) 458-9525
Website: https://robinlearningsystems.com/
Website: https://www.musicmadeeasier.com/
Facebook page: https://www.facebook.com/robinlitster.johnson
LinkedIn Page: https://www.linkedin.com/in/robinlitsterjohnson/
Instagram: https://www.instagram.com/rllj1085/

UNLEASH YOUR
INNER GOLDILOCKS™
BY DR. KASTHURI HENRY, PHD

To the casual reader, Goldilocks[66] is just another imaginative bedtime story. I was never a casual reader. Reading was my sole connection to the universe that was locked out to me as a young girl whose reality was the hopelessness of a bloody war. Reading and reflecting was a magical place of escape and transformation. It is the place that taught me to dream, never give up, never settle for anything that did not sit well with my soul. Reading allowed me to believe I will build a life my heart desired because I have a heart, mind, body, and soul that could work together to take a road least travelled.

The magic of Goldilocks to me was not the little girl safely reuniting with her parents and promising to be a good little obedient child. I was a curious dreamer who understood that the adults do not always get things right. If they did, how come I had to grow up in a war zone where going to school was a life-or-death endeavor? How come the adults who told us to treat everyone with love and respect carried race-based anger, hate, and fear? No, the adults around me did not have it right and the adults in the world outside of my

---

[66]   Robert Southey (1837). *Goldilocks and the Tree Bears.*

island home did not care enough to put kindness and compassion first to make my world safe. In my child's mind, adults had it all wrong and I had to figure out a way to get things just right! Yes, *I was fueled by my own self-appointed mission of getting things just right, and that was the message I got from Goldilocks.*

Maximizing Power of Influence

Research shows that we can each only influence three levels[67] from where we are on any issue. Our three degrees of influence therefore becomes our sphere of influence power. Since every issue can range from the right extreme to the left extreme, it stands to reason that a person at the extreme right end can only influence three levels towards the center. A person at the extreme left end can also only influence three levels towards the center. What if a person takes in multiple perspectives, understands the issue at hand from various vantage points, and centers their thinking? Could they not then show up at the left or right of center? In such a situation, that person can influence three levels towards their right, three levels towards their left, and all those who are in the center, thus geometrically multiplying their power of influence.

Roget's 21st Century thesaurus defines influence as "a personal and unofficial power derived from deference of others to one's character, ability, or station; it may be exerted unconsciously or may operate through persuasion."[68] Unlike position power, influence power is sustainable and not predicated on the authority and control of the job title. Influence is what allows us to drive results and bring about the change we seek through our convincing abilities. If my ability to convince others to bring about meaningful results to further my interest is in the palm of my hands, why would I not grab it?

Goldilocks embodies the ability to see the extremes and choose centeredness. Think about every polarizing issue we face today. How much more pleasant would solving issues be if we had the ability for perspective taking? How prudent would my go-to-market strategy be if my target market was Sri Lankan women living in the US? If I become so myopic that I exclude everyone who is different, can I

---

[67] Nicholas A. Christakis (2009). *Connected: The Surprising Power of Our Social Networks and How They Shape Our Lives.* https://sociology.yale.edu/publications/connected-surprising-power-our -social-networks-and-how-they-shape-our-lives

[68] *Roget's 21st Century Thesaurus,* Third Edition Copyright (2013). https://www.thesaurus.com/ browse/influence#:~:text=Influence

even build a viable business? My inner Goldilocks allows me to assess my target market from a needs-and-wants perspective, allowing me to strategically compete for the total market share by influencing the buying decision. My ability to influence others becomes my financial destiny.

Centered on Purpose

The Zuzunaga Venn Diagram of Purpose[69] illustrates how each of our purpose sits at the centeredness of

1. What I love

2. What I am good at

3. What the world needs

See the power of centering on purpose? My purpose allows me to put my heart and soul into what I do, showcases my exceptional ability to do it, and meets a real need in the marketplace. That means, I find fulfillment and drive my economic engine while continually developing my skills to be best in class.

Goldilocks' approach to getting it just right gives me the mindset to establish my purpose and live a fulfilled life, by design. There are no accidents in life. There are choices and resulting consequences. When people meet me, they assume I am successful because I was lucky and affluent. How lucky is a child born into a warzone? How lucky is that child to have to escape the atrocities, build a life in a new country without parents while raising siblings at the age of sixteen? Success is about purposefully designing life and authentically living that purpose. In my #1 International Best Seller, *Ennobled for Success, From Civil War to a US CFO*[70], I share my introspective journey supported by strangers around the world who had the courage to love me and influence my journey. I played the long game, patiently laid the foundation, and strategically took the necessary steps guided by my unwavering faith that the universe would rise up to meet me, if I walked in my purpose.

---

[69] Andres Zuzunaga. The Zuzunaga Venn Diagram of Purpose. How The Andrés Zuzunaga Venn Diagram Become Ikigai (ikigaitribe.com)
[70] Dr. Kasthuri Henry (2020). *Ennobled for Success, From Civil War to a US CFO*. https://www.amazon.com/Ennobled-Success-Civil-War-CFO-ebook/dp/B08LCN258T

What happed to me did not define me. What happened to me helped me build my resiliency and prepared me for success, because I embraced the Goldilocks spirit and took the lessons to continually center my perspectives. Because I never showed up too hot or too cold, because I mastered the art of influencing others. I never compromised my purpose for all the money in the world. I built a brand and lasting relationships that continue to sustain me. *Purpose is the true north that prevents one from getting lost. It is the lighthouse that brings me back to what matters when I get lost in the rough seas of cutthroat business.*

In his book *Good to Great,* Jim Collins applies the concept of purpose to organizations[71]. Through case studies and strategy mappings he explains why some companies make the leap to success while most others fail. Centering on purpose is not just a success factor for an individual; it is a necessary right of passage for a business seeking sustained competitive advantage. Think about Walgreens as a business. They are not providing pharmacy services; they are "at the corner of happy and healthy,"[72] purposefully serving their target market.

Striking a Balance with Individualism and Collectivism

Individualism and collectivism are two extreme ends of a personal cultural dimension7. Some societies are culturally prone to individualism while others are prone to collectivism. Neither is good or bad but when singularly employed, can bring about lasting damage. What do I mean by this? If I live in a society that believes that only individualism matters and everyone solely focuses on themselves, can that be a truly functional society? "Only I matter and no one else matters" is a self-fulfilling prophecy of isolation, loneliness, and unsupported life. How can such individuals work as a team for a company? How can such people build and sustain a democracy that has a pre-requisite of "we the people"? The other extreme end is collectivism where we matter as a group, and no one has a unique identity. This too is not sustainable in the long run, for work or society. Where does self-motivation come from? What about personal pride, personal development, and personal responsibility?

---

[71] Jim C. Collins (2001). *Good to Great: Why Some Companies Make the Leap...And Others Don't.* https://www.amazon.com/dp/B0058DRUV6/ref=dp-kindle-redirect?_encoding=UTF8&btkr=1
[72] Ibid.

Goldilocks reminds us to find the balance between the two. In his *Cultural Dimensions Theory*, Geert Hofstede[73] explains how finding the centeredness to embody both individualism and collectivism helps a nation and organization thrive. *Polarizing and making a binary choice of individualism or collectivism only results in decline and failure, as we have learned during the global pandemic. Lasting success comes when we can embrace our own uniqueness and develop our individualism without losing sight of the need to be a collective human society that must work together for shared prosperity.*

The Sweet Spot Between Masculinity and Femininity

Masculinity and femininity are not gender identifiers. Rather, they are cultural dimensions that define how a society and organization shows up. Geert Hofstede[74] places masculinity and femininity at two ends of a spectrum where the former is results- and outcome-oriented, while the latter is nurturing and human-centric. We function in a world built by men with rules made by men. Always do more, drive better results, be quick and deliver more profits. Who is doing all this? People are the necessary ingredient in all this but where is the consideration for the human condition? The Great Resignation[75] is reminding us that organizations have compromised the human factor far too often, that organizational behavior and recruitment strategies need to transform to attract and retain talent that builds success.

Neither masculinity nor femininity is bad. They are both necessary. However, they are necessary in the right proportions to find the right balance. Attracting, nurturing, developing, and retaining talent are feminine capabilities necessary to drive masculinity-based results, profits, and business success. Goldilocks reminds us not to be too masculine or too feminine. They are two sides of the same coin and getting the balance just right is the key to building the right culture. The wrong culture will destroy strategy all day, every day leading to business challenges, as we see all around us today. Who would have believed making

---

[73]   Geert Hofstede (1980). *Cultural Dimensions Theory.* https://corporatefinanceinstitute.com/resources/knowledge/other/hofstedes-cultural-dimensions-theory/
[74]   Ibid.
[75]   Gary Drenik (2022). *Forbes* "The Great Resignation Defined 2021: Here's How to Attract, Retain And Engage Employees In 2022." https://www.forbes.com/sites/garydrenik/2022/01/11/the-great-resignation-defined-2021-heres-how-to-attract-retain-and-engage-employees-in-2022/?sh=29e39e3d423a

kindness a priority in the workplace[76] would be the human condition outcome of the global pandemic?

Continually Seeking the Center by Design

Systematically building the power of influence, establishing a purpose-filled life, continually developing and re-aligning that life to keep purpose in perspective, honing the art of embracing individualism while leveraging the value of collectivism, and striking the balance of masculinity and femininity to drive results by lifting up others is the complex adaptive process for success. Just like a well-made sauce, no one ingredient is apparent, but the perfect blend makes the journey look like effortless magic. I know this because I have taken a conscious life journey to unleash my inner Goldilocks. This was never a straight road to present day success, but a meandering, trial-and-error-filled, tenacious undertaking with the help and support of countless blind-spot watchers who have polished me to my present-day brilliance. I know I have much more polishing to undergo and hence my journey continues.

Successful businesses seek and attract leaders who can influence change through innovation and collaborative success. *A leadership team that is capable of being centered and harnessing the power of influence will be far more successful in the long run than organizations that have leaders in name only who exert their positional power to force the outcomes they desire.* When an organization is ennobled for success it embodies a culture demonstrating influence power rooted in purpose balancing

- Individualism with Collectivism: Individualism aspect of our self-motivation and single-minded pursuit needs to be balanced with collectivism aspect of building relationships and leveraging those relationships for success.
- Masculinity with Femininity: Masculinity aspect of our personality that drives results ought to be balanced with the femininity aspect of establishing sustainability for nurturing progress.

---

[76] Dr. Pragya Agarwal (2019). *Forbes.* "Making Kindness a Priority in the workplace." https://www.forbes.com/sites/pragyaagarwaleurope/2019/08/26/making-kindness-a-priority-in-the-workplace/?sh=68b445a38f45

This success must be cultivated and realigned as the business evolves and the environment changes. A continuous improvement mindset with a willingness to plan, do, check, and act to remain true to the strategic purpose, shaped by organizational culture centered on leadership influence is the blueprint for developing agents of change[77]. *The agents of change are the catalyst for building sustained competitive advantage, the economic goal of any business. It is imperative to understand that this economic goal only becomes a reality when leading with the soul to ennoble the stakeholders is made possible[78] by creating the conditions to unleash the inner Goldilocks.*

To continue the ennobling of business, I have embarked on bringing forward my podcast *Unleash Your Inner Goldilocks™, How to Get It Just Right* and made it available on Transforming with Dr. Kas Henry - YouTube. The Goldilocks Book Series will continue to share up concepts and framework to facilitate the continuous improvement mindset to tirelessly ennobling business for success.

Wisdom Gained from the Journey to Ennoble Business

1. Centering on Purpose lays the foundation for economic prosperity while authentically allowing for a fulfilling life.

2. Understanding and channeling the power of influence leads to sustained strategic success with mindful stakeholder relationships.

3. Balancing individualism with collectivism while embracing the sweet spot between masculinity and femininity is the secret to establishing the right human condition for ennobling business for success.

---

[77] Dr. Kasthuri Henry (2012). *Strategic Finance. The FP&A Squad: Financial Agents of Change.* https:// kashenry.com/wp-content/uploads/2020/06/FPA-Squad-Financial-Agents-for-Change-04_2012_ henry.pdf
[78] Dr. Kasthuri Henry (2009). *Strategic Finance. Leading with Your Soul.* https://kashenry.com/ wp-content/uploads/2020/06/LeadingWithYourSoul-36352809-Feb2009-Vol90-Issue8.pdf

Dr. Kasthuri Henry, PhD, is driven by her mission of *Building to Last and Ennobling for Success.* Her ability to understand the importance of first developing the *being* and then bringing that authentic self to all the *doing* makes her a sought-after member of Forbes Coaches Council. She is an accomplished professional who trains organizations and coaches individuals across the world to grow with mindfulness, demonstrating good governance to balance the interest of the individual, organization, and society for sustained mutual prosperity

Dr. Kas shares her wisdom-filled lessons to help others live an ennobled, empowered, and positive life by drawing from her life journey starting with a civil war to becoming a US CFO in her #1 International Best Seller *Ennobled for Success: From Civil War to a US CFO.* Her recent publication *The Resiliency Playbook* that helps readers take a guided journey of self-discovery to building a resilient life also became a #1 International Bestseller.

Dr. Kas is the CEO of **KasHenry Inc.** and the Founder of **Ennobled for Success ™ Institute**. Her business change management, financial strategy, business process improvement, and leadership acumen include global acquisition of the Duracell Brand by Warren Buffet from P&G, standing up as the global leader of L&D and Financial Processes, transforming the Chicago Teachers Pension Fund as the CFO, and more. A graduate school professor, she continues to transform students representing the US military, public safety, private sector, and nonprofit sectors via Southern Illinois University, DeVry University, and North Park University.

A centered approach to solving life's challenges is the theme of her weekly international podcast *Unleash your Inner Goldilocks ™: How to Get It Just Right.*

Website: www.kashenry.com
Email: kas@kashenry.com
LinkedIn: https://www.linkedin.com/in/dr-kasthuri-henry-phd-mba-ctp-6-sigma-black-belt-2028b06/
Instagram: https://www.instagram.com/henrykasthuri/

Facebook: https://www.facebook.com/DrKasHenry
Twitter: https://twitter.com/DrKasthuri
YouTube: Transforming with Dr. Kas Henry - YouTube

CLOSING THOUGHTS

Business is run by people, to serve people, and is facilitated by people. All stakeholders of all businesses are human. That makes human skills the secret sauce for business success. In an era of super specialized technical skills, the human skills have gone unaddressed and undeveloped through the educational process as well as professional development processes. Ignoring it is no longer an option when empathy and resiliency are the two highly sought-after workplace capabilities today.

Human capital is at the foundation of innovation, continuous process improvement, and business sustainability. Human capital drives business processes and customer service resulting in financial success. This makes *human capital the root cause of the sustained value creation effect of business*. Any business that seeks effective long-term economic success must be willing to invest in its human capital and cultivate an environment suitable to bring out the best in its people. Just like there is no beef stew in the absence of beef, there is no business success without employees shaping that success. Employees need to be influenced and led with humanity to bring out the best in them. We have laid out a road map for organizations to make this connection between its people and its success by developing the ability to

1. *Inspire* the human spirit so each soul feels valued and could live its full potential.
2. *Ignite* the sense of purpose to mindfully build a fulfilling life.
3. *Influence* by design to thrive and leave a legacy of ennobling.

It is going to take an all-hands-on-deck approach to turn things around and realign businesses to show up and engage with humanity. The insights and human skills demonstrated in this anthology are part of the tool kit to help in that recalibration journey. *Organizational leadership mindfully embracing these practices and building the organizational muscle memory to create a culture of human excellence will be a long yet rewarding shared journey.* I am grateful that we have taken that first step together as authors, readers, and committed business leaders.

Please look for the accompanying Journal that is expected to be released in early 2023 for additional practical tips in shaping this ennobling journey. The prequel to this anthology is my #1 International Best *Seller Ennobled for Success, from Civil War to a US CFO* and *The Gratitude Journal*, both available on Amazon. *Resiliency Playbook* is another relevant book from my collection to help build a resiliently ennobling business.

Transform with Dr. Kas is a YouTube channel filled with human capability development guidance and conversations with experts to serve as video content library for learning and development.

Ennobled for Success ™ Institute provides further learning and development opportunities as well as coaching to enrich your professional and organizational success.

Join the Ennobling Movement and sign-up at www.kashenry.com for updates and information.

Ennobled for Success: From Civil War to a US CFO takes you through a conscious journey within, for a self-exploration to discover wisdom-filled lessons to support you in living an ennobled, empowered, and positive life.

The book helps you connect with your BEING to purposefully channel your DOING so the light in you could shine. Seeing life through the perspective of gratitude while igniting the process of ennobling to embody noble qualities of kindness, compassion, and empathy as a pathway to leadership and success is an extraordinary road least travelled. This is an unapologetically authentic road map to meaningful success.

THE GRATITUDE
JOURNAL

Dr. Kotchut Henry, PhD, CTP

The Gratitude Journal provides fifty-two weeks of reflective exercises to facilitate your transformational journey and adopt the ennobling road for your own success. This journal contains the opportunity to capture: (1) The week's experience (1a) What happened (1b) How it impacted me (1c) Why I am grateful, and (2) The week's self-reflection. As you begin your journey of gratitude, keep an open mind, become aware of your surroundings, develop the ability to see with your heart, and build the courage to be vulnerable to strangers.

Step into your purpose. Embrace a life of being ennobled. As you take charge of your destiny and navigate towards your success, maintain perspective and find your inner joy. Keep the faith that the universe will rise up to meet you because it is perfectly in tune with the energy you create around you.

The Resiliency Playbook aims to be your practical hands-on guide to a self-discovery journey. It helps you to first identify your limitations and then expand upon them to intentionally thrive.

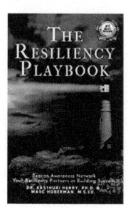

The only constant in life is change. Without resiliency, navigating the speed and volume of change would be simply daunting. The BAN Plan introduced in this book is expected to:

1. Facilitate the identification of the *Basic* realities of your current challenges
2. Formulate the necessary *Adjustments* to successfully navigate through your challenges
3. Implement the *New* game plan to fully live your life purpose

It is our hope that we help you push your boundaries to lead an evolving life at home, school, and work; to not just live, but thrive with purpose as you continually grow as a whole person.

Work in a functional society is performed across its three pillars, namely state (government), market (commerce), and civil society. Family is the fundamental building block of society with workers and other stakeholders coming from their respective homes to engage across state, market, and civil society. Work-life balance is a traditional concept attempting to distribute time for paid work and life. This is a masculine construct that fails to consider the feminine contributions. A refractive thinker sees the flaw in this construct and understands that work is comprised of paid and unpaid work that ought to be equitably budgeted with respect to time. Once the paid and

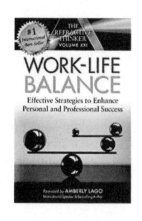

unpaid work are addressed, then life ought to be harmonized with work, because balancing is not possible with disparate requirements placed on people based on their respective genders. Data shows that 75% of the unpaid work totaling up to 11 billion hours a day is carried out by women of the world while men focus mainly on paid work. In the absence of women and their work, life would be non-viable. Therefore, work-life balance needs to be replaced with harmonizing life, to balance the burdens of paid and unpaid work, including total contributions of women.

ACKNOWLEDGEMENTS

T his anthology is a testament to the joy and beauty of an international co-creative process. The lived experience of bringing the anthology forward would not be possible without the authors being value congruent with the purpose of Ennobling Business for Success. The willingness to expand their perspectives to collaborate with agility, stay the course of the book project to honor the timeline, and remain true to their authenticity speaks to the human skills each author embodies. My heart is filled with gratitude for the trust and openness of each chapter author to lean in for the greater good and help co-create a truly meaningful book to enhance the human skill development in our global workplace.

A special note of gratitude to Arjun Nagendran, Co-Founder, Mursion, for the powerful foreword tying the realities of the workplace to the impact of this anthology.

No meaningful journey is taken alone. Our co-creative journey was facilitated by our teams, communities, families, friends, and support systems who believed in this initiative and invested in our shared success.

Bringing forward a collection of work, such as this, in electronic, print, and audio format requires an array of talent, immense coordination, and deep skills in a variety of areas. My publishing and marketing teams are the spokes of the wheel that keeps the forward momentum going and I could not imagine a better team to work with!

The universe is unfolding as it should and the energy field around me to guide this important ennobling work comes from the divine power present within and around me. This divine within me is also within every one of you. I acknowledge this divinity within all of us and am filled with hope that its power will help us build a better world and workplace that befits each of us.

REVIEWS

"The global pandemic has further enhanced the importance of our roles in human resources and as leaders. Retaining great employees starts with having great and caring managers. Each author in this book does a superb job of highlighting this importance by giving concrete examples of how to take care of yourself as well as your employees. Each chapter ends by summarizing three key points, allowing for an easy read and reference for the impactful future work."
- *Mike Taney*, Chief Human Resources Officer, Duracell – A Berkshire Hathaway Company

"Push everything to the side because this is the book you have been waiting for. A highly relevant tome of useful thought and action for our world today. Dr. Kasthuri Henry has captured a wealth of wisdom from valuable experts who go beyond the magic eye picture facade of a digital world to a deeper level, addressing the human side because, after all, 'business is run by people, to serve people, and is facilitated by people.'
It has synthesized a wealth of expertise in well-constructed perspectives to direct us as individuals and organizations for an ennobled future. Bravo to all involved."
- *Dr. Louise Mahler*. International Speaker, Executive Team Mentor & Executive Coach - Australia. https://louisemahler.com.au/

"A meaningful life is crafted not through 'what' you do but through discovering 'why' you do it. *Ennobling Business for Success* is a truly brilliant anthology that captures the essence of living a purpose-driven life and career through the power of human ties and collaboration. Packed with practical wisdom and actionable strategies, this book is a must-read for all those who seek to tap into their full potential and create their own unique definition of success."
- *Nim Gholkar*. Author, Speaker, Life Coach, Australia. www.nimsniche.com

"Living purpose is possible! The compilation of personal and professional stories across experiences and cultures leaves the reader with hope. Hope that they too can find a link between personal and professional purposes and live it out loud. Dr. Henry has created a must-read for those struggling to find meaning in the business world."
- *Charlotte Allen*, PhD. CEO, Rebel Success for Leaders, USA. https://rebelsuccessforleaders.com/

"This anthology is a genuine testimony that evolving together is possible, whatever our differences in our cultures, educations, backgrounds, and life choices. Each author brings their pearl of wisdom and encouragement so that each aspirant can become a transcendent leader. With a balance between our individual and collective consciousness, a thriving world seems reachable: these writers, themselves leaders, show us the way with creativity, genius, generosity, and authenticity; their respective shared experiences illustrate their talk divinely. Greatly recommended to read and receive a boost of hope and inspiration!"
- *Sophie Roumeas.* Therapist in hypnosis & family constellation, author – France. www.sophieroumeas.com

"Kasthuri Henry has gathered a collection of stories rife with lessons to illuminate a path to more ethical, positive leadership. Each chapter is a piece in a larger tapestry that provides a clear picture of what it takes to lead in ways that inspire others and create goodness at an individual and organizational level. This is an essential read for today's leaders."
- *Liz Corcoran.* Senior Vice President, Design, Impact Performance Group, USA. www.impactpg.com

"An extremely powerful anthology with each chapter inspiring anew with rich knowledge, experience, and personal growth of the authors. The authors bring fresh perspectives, lived experiences, and practical tips to the reader. In each juncture, intense and powerful actions of gratitude, appreciation, and giving are always present. Authors reflect on the technological and globalization challenges as well as changes humanity constantly face. Working collaboratively as a wholesome community is the recipe for success as the global pandemic has shown us. We have our subliminal potential to tap into and thrive."
- *Cruz Oliverio Gamez.* Managing Director, Gama Financial Services Ltd, Belize. cruz@gama.bz

"This collection of carefully and brilliantly chosen people, and meticulously thought through chapters, written with the sole purpose of Inspiring, Igniting, and Influencing organizations and individuals, is in itself a very clever masterstroke. Its arrival and timing is a direct response to deep spiritual and integrated shifts taking place right now in our hurting world. The planet itself, communities and individuals so need to be ignited and influenced to now live differently. We are being invited to be more and to live with far more awareness and a sense of true inner abundance."
- *Catherine Rolt*. Integrated Chinese Medical Consultant, CEO of UnRavel Dis-Ease Naturally Ltd, UK. www.UnRaveldis-EaseNaturally.com

"This book is life-changing as it shares soulful, moral guidance and experiences from individuals from different backgrounds and occupations. It inspires and motivates the reader to strive for fulfillment in life whilst utilizing evidential practices with a focus on human beings at the center of the equation. Once personal skills are at its maximum level, professional growth, business, and community output are also maximized, creating a rewarding experience filled with quality, and purpose. This intellectual growth helps in the evolution of the person in leadership, influencing the employees and the community who are all beneficiaries of an ennobling journey."
- *Anna Rachel Montejo*. Attorney at Law in Belize, a.rachel.montejo@gmail.com

"*Ennobling Business for Success* is a book that disrupts the current paradigm of how business is done. Reading the perspective of Dr. Kasthuri along with the authors led me to the conclusion that people no longer want a separation between work and life. There is simply life, and we have finally decided that suffering in our work is no longer tolerable. This book is not one to be read once and put on a shelf. With the abundance of insight and concrete actions the authors offer, it is a valuable tool designed to propel the reader forward into an *ennobled* future."
- *Linda C Heeler, PCC*. USA. www.LiveInspiredLifeCoaching.com

"*Ennobling Business for Success* is a must-read collection of inspiring thought leadership from many authors. Each chapter comprises of engaging topics of human connections and purpose. It lays out a blueprint of how to create a brighter future in business while helping us become better in our everyday lives."
- *Hieu Bui, MD MBA FACHE*. USA. https://www.linkedin.com/in/hieu-bui-md-mba-fache-572b33a4/

"The ability to identify one's own purpose and build it as a leadership skillset can be a great challenge to most. Harnessing these skills as our own individual superpowers, making us who we are, is invaluable. In this book, the authors individually and collectively help you to learn more from their respective non-linear journey and the value they bring in life and work."
- *Kevyn Rustici*. Area Vice President - Strategic Human Capital Consultant

"What a wonderful collection of authors and wisdom gathered in *Ennobling Business for Success*! This book is a powerful combination of inspiration and insights, shared through the eyes of delightfully diverse and successful individuals. What makes this so impactful is the holistic approach to the topics providing authentic insights from life, faith, failures, support, lessons, connections, and much more. Each chapter is a gift that helps you understand and unfold your own success by tapping into WHO you are, HOW you think, and WHAT you bring into the world. It's a must-read! "
- *Barbara Miller*. Leadership & Life Coach, and Author. Mighty Inspiration, LLC, USA. www.mightyinspiration.com

"Individually, we are one drop, but together we are an ocean," a quote from this magnificent anthology best summarized the powerful and effective business strategies weaved together cohesively by this incredible team of authors. I would recommend this inspiring book to anyone seeking new, effective blueprints to establish their business, or to move forward with one in a post-pandemic world."
- *MacKenzie Nelson*, #1 International Best Selling Author, https://www.mackenziekaynelson.com

"*Ennobled Business for Success* brings transformational leadership into the world of corporate America. Its authors represent STEM majors and corporate executives and deliver a refreshing perspective of what is missing in corporate leadership in the post-pandemic workplace. An enlightening read that sources input not often heard from our right brain colleagues."
- *Maureen Ryan Blake*. Maureen Ryan Blake Media Production, USA.

Made in the USA
Monee, IL
18 June 2023

35921585R00079